THE POWER in A LINK

OPEN DOORS, CLOSE DEALS, AND CHANGE THE WAY YOU DO BUSINESS USING LINKEDIN

DAVID GOWEL

WILEY

John Wiley & Sons, Inc.

Published by John Wiley & Sons, Inc., Hoboken, New Jersey.
Published simultaneously in Canada.

For general information on our other products and services or for technical support, please contact our Customer Care Department within the United States at (800) 762-2974, outside the United States at (317) 572-3993 or fax (317) 572-4002.

Wiley publishes in a variety of print and electronic formats and by print-on-demand. Some material included with standard print versions of this book may not be included in e-books or in print-on-demand. If this book refers to media such as a CD or DVD that is not included in the version you purchased, you may download this material at http://booksupport.wiley.com. For more information about Wiley products, visit www.wiley.com.

Library of Congress Cataloging-in-Publication Data:
Gowel, Dave, 1980-
  The power of a link: open doors, close deals, and change the way you do business using LinkedIn/
Dave Gowel.
     p. cm.
  Includes index.
  ISBN 978-1-118-13467-2 (pbk.); ISBN 978-1-118-17594-1 (ebk); ISBN 978-1-118-17595-8 (ebk);
ISBN 978-1-118-17596-5 (ebk)
  1. LinkedIn (Electronic resource) 2. Business networks—Computer network resources. I. Title.
HD69.S8G69 2012
658.8'72—dc23

                                                                                    2011029145

Printed in the United States of America

10 9 8 7 6 5 4 3 2 1

To the woman who taught me the power of earning social capital through leading by example, seeking first to give, and then to receive. Mom, thank you for all that you've done and all that you are.

Contents

Foreword

I HAVE MADE several significant career changes in my life, including the transition from being a civilian to serving in the military; from the military to the NFL; and from the NFL to commercial real estate. Throughout these diverse careers, I've noticed a common trend relevant to any industry: exceptional relationships lead to exceptional success.

A naval officer is ineffective without his sailors executing tactically. A quarterback cannot score touchdowns without seamless teamwork between linemen who block and receivers who catch. And a broker does not close deals if he does not provide the best service to his clients. The success of these professional relationships is also influenced by the caliber of the players involved. To achieve more than mediocrity, one can hope to be surrounded by remarkable professionals who also perform beyond the call of duty. However, I've found that it is unwise to simply *hope* you will always join teams of remarkable performers who work well together to consistently achieve superior results. Such successful relationships require proactivity, a challenge that the best teams overcome together.

While building exceptional relationships or achieving peak performance once you find them, "hoping" is a common practice many professionals deploy. Dave Gowel has shown me that when used properly, LinkedIn allows professionals to replace hope with decisive action in this context. This tool lets people find key contacts in a mutually beneficial manner, making the resultant business relationships more productive.

I met Dave through his company's work with Jones Lang LaSalle, a firm for which I am currently the executive chairman for the Americas. At the time we met, I was interested in his military background and entrepreneurial spirit. I did not fully appreciate the value that social technologies would play in business. However, I've now learned how Dave's company, RockTech, is helping the world understand how these new technologies make relationship building and management more efficient than ever.

Some believe that our tech-savvy youth are becoming introverted as they spend more and more time interacting with their peers online. However, Dave shows us that the art of communicating and building relationships is now actually *more* effective than any methods my generation had the chance to use, thanks to these new technologies.

In this book, you will learn both the potential power that your current network already contains, as well as how to turn that power into tangible opportunities and warm introductions with the help of LinkedIn.

From one football player, corporate leader, military officer, entrepreneur, chairman, board member, and avid reader to another, this book is well worth the read.

—Roger Staubach
NFL Hall of Fame Quarterback and
Executive Chairman, Americas,
Jones Lang LaSalle

Preface

MY STORY STARTS as a West Point cadet looking to serve my country, become an Army Ranger, see the world, and learn what it really means to be a leader. After leaving the military, I found myself on the unexpected path of watching a social media revolution explode in front of me while teaching on the subject of leadership as an assistant professor at the Massachusetts Institute of Technology (MIT). This allowed me to transition from a West Point graduate and Army Ranger serving in a tank platoon in Baghdad, to a young educator at a world-renowned academic institution, to the CEO of RockTech, a company I cofounded with Mark Rockefeller. All of this occurred in less than six years, in the worst economy of my life, and all before I turned 30. This confluence of learning from the brilliant young minds at Facebook's ground zero (I liaised with Harvard's faculty and administrators from my position at MIT to support the Harvard students participating in our courses), the intellectual curiosity surrounding this revolution at an academic powerhouse, and my entrepreneurial desire to start and lead a civilian enterprise have made me comfortable speaking authoritatively on the currency that made this new "power" possible: social capital.

Having reached my thirtieth birthday while finishing up this book, I don't purport to have decades of industry experience that allow me to sit atop a mountain in the lotus position, posing riddles to my visitors. However, it is because my professional life has been spent between the social media generation and corporate America's current leaders that I can see both perspectives on how each is using these new technologies—and see as well what each is lacking. The latter group struggles to understand why the former so readily shares so much information about themselves publicly and substitutes face-to-face interaction with texting or wall posts. The former group hasn't had as much opportunity to experience the powerful impact that a warm introduction or sage bit of social business intelligence can have on a business deal, career transition, or personal challenge.

Describing the past decade of my life as a whirlwind would be quite the understatement. Between the life-changing experiences of graduating from the United States Military Academy at West Point, earning my Ranger Tab, serving in Iraq, and cofounding and leading two civilian companies, I also orchestrated high-end events for multiple four-star generals in Europe, moved to Boston and grew my network from scratch, taught military leadership to students at MIT and six other schools, was accepted into a master's program at Harvard, and cofounded a successful marketing firm in a recession—all while being in awe of the little trooper my wife and I welcomed into the world in 2008.

Today, I am a CEO, an entrepreneur, and a leader who recognizes that I can achieve nothing without a talented, well-informed, and aligned team executing (and improving upon) my vision. I wrote *The Power in a Link* to help the world see what I've experienced by recognizing that LinkedIn, which so many consider a contact manager or resume site, is so much more than it appears. I'm a walking case study that demonstrates the professional power of this unparalleled business tool. LinkedIn's social map and its accompanying relationship-focused search capability will change business forever, whether you like it or not. In fact, it was my use of LinkedIn that put this book before you today. I used it to request a warm introduction to Anne Smith, a senior executive at one of the world's leading publishing houses of social media books through the following e-mail that I sent one evening to a client and friend:

To: Foote, Richard

Sent: Thursday, February 17, 2011, 7:21 P.M.

Hi Richard: I was passed the name of Anne Smith today by my writer as your name popped up as being connected with Anne in LinkedIn (www.linkedin.com/in/anneelizabethsmith). Do you know her well? As we consider if now is the right time to publish my book (given LinkedIn's upcoming IPO), I'd love to invite Anne to our office on the Rockefeller Family Floor at 30 Rock to seek her thoughts on how best we should proceed with my book. Any thoughts you have would be, as always, much appreciated.

—Dave

Because of the social capital I built with Richard, I received this helpful reply early the next morning:

From: Foote, Richard

Sent: Friday, February 18, 2011, 8:48 A.M.

I know her very well. It would not be an understatement to say she has been one of my best friends for almost 40 years (we went to college together). I'll be in the Boston office this after-noon. Send me a note as to when it would be a good time to speak and we can talk about how I can be helpful.

Due to the subsequent meetings this simple request stimulated, I received my contract from John Wiley & Sons to publish this book on April 18: a mere two months after I directly stimulated word of mouth using the knowledge I proactively and swiftly gained through LinkedIn.

About the Author

Dave Gowel is the CEO of RockTech, a board member of the East End House, and founding member of the Kendall Square Association. Dave graduated from West Point, taught at MIT as an assistant professor of military leadership, and served as a U.S. Army Ranger and Armor combat platoon leader in Iraq. Through his successes, Dave earned the title of "LinkedIn Jedi" in *The Boston Globe*.

In addition to the time Dave spends focused on LinkedIn and the platform RockTech has built to enable its adoption, he supports various nonprofit organizations in educational and military causes.

Dave lives with his wife, Julie, and son, Charlie, in Boston, Massachusetts.

You can find more at: www.linkedin.com/in/davidgowel.

Introduction

IT'S A STRANGE feeling . . . being awake while everyone else is asleep.

Although you may not actually be nodding off as you read this, if you're like most of the world, you probably have not yet woken up to the real power of social technology—especially the professional networking site, LinkedIn. It's one thing to know that there's power in this forum; it's another entirely to be able to explain how you *already* use it successfully to close deals. We're going to help you achieve the latter. The core value proposition of LinkedIn to successful professionals is outlined in the sections that follow.

LinkedIn exponentially increases your network *utility*. Most people who think they understand professional social networking tools always agree with me on the first five words of that phrase. In other words, they assume that the more people you have in your network, the greater the likelihood of achieving your professional goals. However, it's not about just having a *bigger* network; it's about getting more *utility* out of that network and saving time as you conduct business without harassing or overcommunicating to professionals. This book will show you how our networks are actually already much bigger than we need them to be to accomplish our goals. The challenge is learning how to extract more out of your network, faster than you have before in order to outpace those who compete for the currently available market share of client prospects, top talent, investors, business partners, and so forth. That is precisely what LinkedIn allows you to do . . . but only if you use it the right way.

LinkedIn is *not* social media. Unlike most LinkedIn books that describe how to get the most out of this social media tool, *The Power in a Link* focuses on extracting the *business* value from LinkedIn in a time-efficient manner. Ironically, it's not the *social* part of *social media* that makes this term a bad descriptor for this technology. Rather, the *media* element of this phrase has made users think that they need to actively send out transmissions to as many people as possible, as often as they can and *be in a conversation* about their personal brand for LinkedIn to be used effectively. This is not the case. In fact, according to the most successful professionals with whom I've worked, too much messaging and conversation, solely for the sake of conversation, is considered to be unprofessional noise—not something that promotes your business goals, but that actually degrades your ability to achieve them.

What You Can Expect to Find in *The Power in a Link*

There have been many books written about LinkedIn, and most provide tips and tricks for things like building Profiles and expanding your network. Although *The Power in a Link* will give you those as well, the major difference between those books and this one is that I'll demonstrate the victories I prescribe for you. I will walk you through how I've met exceptional success using LinkedIn, providing the tactics and etiquette that turns social network theory into tangible business deals. The methods I'll share can help you protect your network's privacy and security while amplifying (not replacing) the traditional methods of real-world networking, lead generation, due diligence, sales cycle shortening, hiring, and making strategic business decisions that you perform every day.

This book sets out to awaken you to the potential of LinkedIn through how-tos and anecdotes. I've inserted some relevant and more detailed biographical anecdotes for your deeper understanding of my journey with LinkedIn (and a bit of enjoyment) along the way. You can choose to either read or skip over these sidebars, depending on your interest in them, without missing out on the thrust of the book.

Another reason I took the time out from leading my business to write this book is my desire to thank and repay some social capital to those key members of my network who have facilitated my successes. These individuals made important introductions, provided significant business intelligence, gave exceptional advice, helped me learn from my mistakes, and became wonderful friends, advisors, clients, and investors. You will read stories about them, some with clear titles and some who may remain incognito for one reason or another, under names like John Awesome. I will also mention and change the names of some folks I've come across who could use some education in social capital, such as Jane NoGood (these individuals' anonymity is for their own protection).

The Power in a Link will show you how social technology tangibly helped me accomplish ambitious professional goals. It will tell the story that led up to the launch of RockTech, the business in which I now enable, scale, and track effective training on LinkedIn usage by employees and their corporations (with more technologies coming soon). You will gain a clear understanding of the way LinkedIn can function as a game-changing business tool for you and those with whom you work on a daily basis.

I'll tell you the story—people say it's colorful—of how I use LinkedIn in the real world to generate significant business success for myself and our clients. I will share the lessons I learned that have led me to where I am now, with the expectation that it will quiet the noise that may be keeping you from understanding how social technology can work for you and your corporation, partnership, office, sole proprietorship, or business division.

I'll walk you through the details of how LinkedIn has been critical to my success and suggest ways your LinkedIn network can help you, as it helped one of my clients at Silicon Valley Bank:

> "David and RockTech have assisted us to close deals by using LinkedIn that we may not otherwise have closed, *totaling over $20 million*. We at SVB have worked with RockTech in multiple capacities including conference speaking roles, workshops, intense training programs and their own software platform (TAP). RockTech is a salient leader in this rapidly evolving industry and we are happy to recommend them."
> **—Mark Gallagher, Senior Vice President, Sales Origination at SVB Financial Group**

What Has Kept the World Fast Asleep?

As I implied in the first sentence of this section, I believe many people have yet to wake up when it comes to effectively using LinkedIn. Exactly what sedative has kept the professional world from awakening to the power of this technology? There are four key parts to this cocktail:

1. **Facebook:** The Facebook eruption confused the world about what LinkedIn truly is and the value it provides. LinkedIn essentially fell into the ever-growing stew of technologies grouped as social media, despite the fact that it predates Facebook. Nowadays, many see LinkedIn as merely "Facebook in a suit." Inviting someone to connect on LinkedIn is often erroneously perceived as the professional equivalent of "friending someone"—a misconception that has caused a devaluation of this technology's true potential.

2. **Nonintuitive behaviors:** LinkedIn is years ahead of the professionals who can best use it to achieve their business goals. Not because LinkedIn is difficult to use, but it's because the social business intelligence LinkedIn provides has never been available, making its real-world usage nonintuitive. The mentality of those who say, "Put my Rolodex onto the Internet so

others can steal the network I've grown? You're crazy!" has left some people thinking that reflecting one's trusted network on LinkedIn is risky, providing hunting grounds for some to poach on the relationships that others have spent a lifetime building. This has even bred contempt for the tool, as well as a false justification for those who like to keep on "status quo-ing." In reality, and from personal interactions with LinkedIn executives, I've learned that the corporation behind this professional network could not be more protective of its users' networks and its platform. In fact, the platform actually serves as an amplifier for those with the highest caliber networks, where they can extract tangible benefits while protecting and even reinforcing their real-world relationships. Professionals have become much more accessible to others in the past decade due to the explosion of online connectivity. But many of the most traditional professionals have fallen into a false sense of security, thinking that by keeping their Rolodexes locked in their desks, they can hide their personal networks from the competition.

3. **Complex and risky:** The population postured to benefit most from LinkedIn consists of the established, business-leading generation of professionals who have been successful *without* LinkedIn for their entire professional careers. They are accustomed to the concept of using relationships to drive business, but they claim to currently do it—and want to continue doing it—"the right way, in the real world, not in cyberspace." Most of these individuals haven't been willing to dive into LinkedIn and try it, even if they get past the first two hurdles. They don't want to test their ability to be quick learners by risking a mistake that could impact their reputation in front of their networks just by trying to get LinkedIn.

4. **The same, but *very* different:** Although LinkedIn's most valuable technical features have not materially changed since launching in 2003, the tangible value that the platform now provides wasn't accessible until recently. This core, valuable

functionality didn't (and won't) exist for its users until the following occurs:

○ LinkedIn itself first reaches a critical mass of many millions of users in a relevant target market.
○ The users seeking value connect to enough of the people they know on LinkedIn, but *only* the people they know.

Because these criteria need to go hand in hand, many tech-savvy early users of LinkedIn found it to be useful but not sufficiently compelling, because the platform didn't have enough users. This caused those innovators to slide into LinkedIn behavior patterns (and be followed by the masses) that bypass the tool's real value. And this real value is what puts LinkedIn on a glide path to revolutionize business.

It is this cocktail of sedatives that causes many of LinkedIn's current and prospective users to struggle when trying to comprehend the concept of mapping their long-standing networks. If these people understood the power here, they would use LinkedIn to activate that untapped value waiting for them just inches beyond their current reach. A metaphor I use to explain this argument compares LinkedIn to a common tool: If LinkedIn is a thousand-blade Swiss Army knife, most people start using a few of its blades, the ones that they can easily figure out; they don't look deeper into the tool because they find value in and start to use those first few blades. However, many people are using the blades ineffectively, and the majority of users aren't even using the most valuable ones (especially since the best "LinkedIn blades" don't come presharpened).

How I Ended Up Here, Writing This Book

It has become a passion of mine to help the world understand how to leverage new, misunderstood, and underutilized technologies, with only the first one being that Swiss Army knife that is LinkedIn. But it took a unique journey for me to realize this passion. And most of my accomplishments would not have been achievable without the incredible network and team that I developed, the cultivation of my LinkedIn prowess, and, of course, an over-abundance of caffeine.

Ironically, I first started to learn the value of LinkedIn from my students. While serving in MIT's Reserve Officers' Training Corps (ROTC) program, I was responsible for liaising with the Harvard ROTC students. I was able to teach young leaders at both ends of the city how to transition from Cambridge academia to combat leadership. Since this coincided with Facebook's explosive success, my students, who were among Facebook's first users, gave me daily lessons on using social media. Then, while building my first company in less than ideal economic conditions, I discovered that LinkedIn was the best social networking ally for those challenging times.

Having used this networking tool with our clients since 2007, I've experimented with LinkedIn and other social platforms extensively. I've made some rookie mistakes while using it, but also discovered and built upon the most beneficial, game-changing aspects. I grew a team that consulted and trained on LinkedIn, when we weren't using it ourselves to drive revenue, build market share, and keep our investors willing to invest in our next big idea. Yet unlike other social media experts, we didn't spend our time consulting or training on LinkedIn with a focus on being in more conversations, having a high number of connections, or showing off catchy job titles. In short, we didn't do anything that we didn't think would directly lead to tangible benefits like topline revenue growth, warm lead generation, and measurably faster hiring. It was this business that refined our LinkedIn expertise, informed us of best practices, and empowered us to seize a bigger opportunity for effectively training many more people than just those with whom we could personally interact.

My current company, RockTech, has built the Technology Adoption Platform (TAP), which overlays and integrates with LinkedIn's actual user interface. More generally, TAP is a strategic tool for corporations to provide initial and ongoing technology adoption for their employees in a manner where users learn while actually using that technology. *TAP for LinkedIn* helps people learn the best practices I demonstrate in this book to achieve significant business successes while inside their own LinkedIn Profiles. Our platform allows corporations to empower rather than prey on their employees. Yet the power of our software—as with LinkedIn's—is always rooted in the *human behaviors* outside cyberspace that are enabled and amplified because of it.

Because of my success with LinkedIn usage, I earned warm introductions to LinkedIn founder, Greylock Partner, and industry icon Reid Hoffman, as well as many of LinkedIn's executives, cofounders, and investors. LinkedIn has passed us business, introduced us as a reliable source to the *New York Times* and *Fox News*, showcased my story to its employees and users by featuring me in their 100 million-user marketing campaign, invited me to speak at an internal company panel discussion, and supported TAPs launch by signing a coveted application programming interface (API) agreement with RockTech. I was even invited to sit in the front row at a LinkedIn-sponsored event that hosted the President of the United States and—most importantly—LinkedIn has built the professional network that changed my life.

Keep in mind that we had no incentive to choose LinkedIn over any other social networking platform. As other tools emerge, RockTech will master them and deliver adoption products in addition to those offered for LinkedIn (since we don't see LinkedIn falling from the forefront of this industry any time soon). We recognize and explain that LinkedIn is not the be-all and end-all business tool. Our team uses it to amplify the actions we've performed before. In addition to LinkedIn, we focus on finding and simplifying the best yet most misunderstood technologies so that you can more easily generate and measure business successes.

For me, using LinkedIn began as a way to generate leads and gain key introductions for my first business: a Cambridge-based marketing firm called Clearly Creative. I soon realized that the domain expertise surrounding social technology was going to become much bigger than just a resource to grow the marketing firm. I've progressed from a guy who made fun of social media (you'll hear a story about my friend Amos later in Chapter 5) to a LinkedIn Jedi (dubbed as such by the *Boston Globe*'s Scott Kirsner).

Having spent these past few years of my life clarifying Linked-In's power to various corporate audiences, I've come to realize that it's truly all about the individual. Despite this tool's breadth of use for those in the business world—including lead generation, hiring, job searching, closing deals, shortening sales cycles, marketing, and search engine optimization (SEO)—LinkedIn isn't going to be game-changing for everybody.

Because LinkedIn allows you to amplify the value of your relationships and your personal brand, it is most powerful for those hardworking, value-producing, ethical individuals who are not getting as much out of their networks as they think they deserve. These people often think, "If more people knew about me and the exceptional work I'm doing, I would achieve my business goals much faster than I am now."

On the other hand, if your efforts or brand haven't positively impacted anybody else, LinkedIn will only make you more aware of that fact. If Jane NoGood is unethical and lazy, nobody in her network is going to want to make introductions for her or provide her with the valuable social business intelligence she seeks, no matter how many connections she can amass. Unfortunately for Ms. NoGood, one of the things that LinkedIn *cannot* do is generate fools that will hire bad employees or lazy service providers, buy poor products, or invest in weak entrepreneurs.

I ask you to think about this question as you join me on this journey: "What if a world existed where you could dramatically reduce the time it takes to find clients, employees, investors, service providers, or other business partners by using, not abusing, valuable, trust-based relationships?"

Keep this question in mind as you read, and you'll also begin to understand how LinkedIn is making this ultraefficient professional connectivity a reality for you.

It's a hefty task to enlighten the world on the ways LinkedIn is going to change business despite the four hurdles mentioned that have stood in its way thus far. Therefore, we'll start with a basic discussion of the commonly misunderstood idea of social capital. Without this understanding, I would not have been able to start and grow a successful marketing firm in the most difficult economy since the Great Depression. I also wouldn't be leading a company with Mark Rockefeller as a friend, investor, and business partner. And I certainly wouldn't be here, writing this book.

So I ask you to join me, because if you choose to hit the snooze button on this wake-up call, your competitors who react to this alarm will be the first to thank you.

Introduction Summary

- My story is used to showcase the behaviors inside and outside LinkedIn that enable tangible business success with this tool.
- Choosing not to use LinkedIn helps your competitors to succeed.
- Earliest adopters have misunderstood LinkedIn because: (1) Facebook has caused mass confusion about its value; (2) the behaviors that make LinkedIn data useful in the real world are not intuitive; (3) those who don't want to accidentally misuse a feature that impacts personal networks perceive LinkedIn as complex and therefore risky; and (4) there was a multiyear delay for a critical mass of people to join LinkedIn, which ultimately made its true value available, but only when users connect to the right people.

PART

1

Why Wake Up?

1

Engaging in the Social Capital Trade

SOCIAL CAPITAL IS a term you've probably heard before and one that I will use often throughout this book. It doesn't come with an official definition from Webster's Dictionary . . . yet. Unlike financial capital, social capital can't be bought. It takes time and trust to earn, maintain, and use (not abuse) social capital. Yet, once you've harnessed and mastered its power, it can become one of the most valuable assets for both your personal and professional lives.

Wikipedia defines *social capital* as a sociological concept used in business, economics, organizational behavior, political science, public health, and the social sciences in general to refer to connections within and between social networks.[1] *Bowling Alone* author Robert Putnam captured the concept well when he said, "Just as a screwdriver (physical capital) or a college education (human capital) can increase productivity (both individual and collective), so too social contacts affect the productivity of individuals and groups."[2] As an evolution of these definitions, I define social capital as the intangible value Person A assigns to Person B when Person B requests a favor from Person A (an introduction, a recommendation, provision of business intelligence, and so on).

The building up, cashing in, and exchanging of social capital makes the world of business go round. These transactions require trust, integrity, and credibility to generate the social capital, facilitate exchanges, or increase value; yet social capital is not an asset that is commonly measured by most professionals when evaluating themselves or others. It's also not measured when most businesses are valued—even though it should be.

To help clarify the idea of trading in social capital as I see it, I highlight my relationship with Bill Aulet, a senior lecturer and the managing director of the MIT Entrepreneurship Center. I have established and maintained a professional relationship with Bill after being introduced to him by one of our mutual trusted colleagues at MIT (more about the legendary Peter Kurzina later). Bill was not an easy guy to pin down for our first meeting, but when I finally got in front of him and showed him what I was doing with LinkedIn, he understood it immediately and became one of my biggest champions (you may have noticed his quote on the back of this book). I had therefore laid the basic foundation on which I could build social capital with him.

To take it a step further, let's say I discovered through LinkedIn that Bill was connected to John BoardMember, who serves on the Board of Directors of a company in my target market. Because I have that solid social capital foundation with Bill, I would feel comfortable asking him to introduce me to BoardMember (that is, if I felt I provided a compelling and relevant value proposition that Bill would agree with). Of course, this introduction would have to be meaningful for all parties involved. If Bill had a strong relationship with BoardMember, I am confident that he would consider placing his personal brand at *social capital risk* by providing me that one introduction.

In this case, if I offer any value for BoardMember once we are introduced, a few things happen:

1. Bill's social capital store increases with me (I owe him for making the introduction).

2. Bill's social capital store increases with BoardMember (Bill made an introduction that ultimately produced some sort of value for BoardMember).
3. I lay the foundation to build social capital with BoardMember.

This example illustrates the importance of making valuable introductions that benefit everyone involved. Had I wasted Board-Member's time by making a bad impression on him (for example, if I tried to sell him something he didn't want or talked about myself without listening to his interests) instead of providing some kind of value to him, I would make both myself and Bill look bad. BoardMember wouldn't want to continue a relationship with me, and Bill certainly wouldn't be making any more introductions on my behalf—since he traded in social capital by essentially saying, "John, by introducing you to Dave Gowel, I'm investing my time in making this introduction. I'm also risking my personal brand in tying my name to the potential success (or lack thereof) of your overall experience with Dave."

So, hypothetically, Bill chose to make this introduction as a savvy businessman, with the expectation that this investment of time and risk of his personal brand would yield:

1. The personal enjoyment that he gets by introducing two people he knows and likes (contrasted to the personal displeasure of making a cold call in an attempt to build relationships for himself or his business).
2. The knowledge that BoardMember and Dave will value Bill and his brand more after this successful introduction, thereby raising Bill's social capital account with both parties.

Let's go back to my original request for an introduction from Bill. What if I had e-mailed Bill and asked him to introduce me to not one but four people I wanted to reach for my personal benefit? As a busy and respectable professional, Bill might not even have responded to that e-mail. He would more than likely ignore it, and probably think that I had overstepped my boundaries, pondering, "Who does Gowel think he is? Am I here just to sit around and make introductions for him all day?" And really—who could blame him for thinking this way?

Some of you (the sales professionals out there) may respond, "Well, why not? Why is it so outrageous to ask Bill for four introductions—especially if he respects you and feels comfortable referring you to people on his behalf? Isn't that what effective networking is all about?"

This concept is best explained by relating social capital to social norms. In certain environments, different actions are acceptable to different people. For example, it's perfectly normal in the United States to approach someone and shake hands the first time you are introduced. In other countries, kissing someone on both cheeks the first time you meet is acceptable if you've been introduced by a close mutual contact or family member. But had I given Bill the double cheek treatment the first time I met him, I suspect that the only introduction he would have made for me would have been to his door.

As with social norms, there is a fine line of etiquette that goes along with trading in social capital, both online and offline. It requires that you develop an understanding of your target market's environment, the activities in which they are currently engaged, and what they expect of you. It's not easy, but this is how you can figure out the exchange rate of the social capital that you possess. This, of course, is far more difficult than a monetary exchange: unfortunately, you can't peer into your wallet to find out how much social capital you've lost or gained with a particular person.

Of course, the concept of networking and asking for introductions is nothing new. Techniques like attending networking events, handing out business cards and cold calling have been around long before the existence of LinkedIn. But now that we've entered into this new era of business, LinkedIn is augmenting some of these antiquated ways of spreading word of mouth (WOM). LinkedIn is *not* a complete substitute for more traditional ways of networking. Face-to-face contact, social skills, and a firm handshake are still vital for most people (including me) to achieve the success they seek, and that's not going to disappear. LinkedIn isn't replacing these traditional methods; it is significantly amplifying them.

For example, I attended a networking event to accomplish various goals one summer morning in 2009, one of which required getting in front of highly regarded *Boston Globe* columnist and blogger Scott Kirsner. My goal was to meet Scott, convince him of my LinkedIn prowess through a gratis LinkedIn training session, learn from his critiques, and earn some favorable press (you'll find a more detailed version of why he dubbed me a LinkedIn Jedi later in Chapter 8).

I have built social capital, supplemented by LinkedIn, with many respected business leaders by providing value during my first interaction with them and by being a hardworking person who values integrity. Of course, there are ways other than through LinkedIn to build social capital with people in the real world, many of which just require common sense. In fact, some of these are critical to enable LinkedIn to be effective for you in business, as LinkedIn doesn't obviate the need for human contact. Here are some networking best practices I've found useful that should be used *with*, not instead of, LinkedIn:

1. **Be patient and reasonable:** A few months ago, I was introduced to a guy—we'll call him John Impatient—by a friend who felt we would mutually benefit each other. After I had to reschedule a phone call at the last minute with Impatient for the second time (because of a second unforeseen conflicting event), Impatient decided I wasn't worth the wait. He left a stern message with my assistant saying, "This is the second time Dave's cancelled on me; I'm no longer interested in meeting him." Had Impatient given me the benefit of the doubt, his social capital would have started off high with me, as I would be looking to repay him for the inconvenience I had caused. It just so happened that I had to reschedule with him because I was working on a major business deal from which Impatient could have benefited, had

he not been offended that there was something I had to prioritize above my interaction with him. When people re-schedule on me, I generally assume that they are so busy with the positive things going on in their business that they will be worth the wait. This is especially the case when I am introduced to new contacts by people I trust (mostly thanks to LinkedIn).

2. **Follow up:** Often forgotten in the business world, following up is essential, not only when you want to get introduced for a job, to make a sales pitch, or to ask for a favor, but also *after* you receive fruitful introductions, advice, or favors from people in your network. When trusted colleagues risk their personal brands to introduce you to someone in their networks, it will reinforce your social capital to follow up with that introducer to thank and update them on the meeting's success. If people invest their time to give you advice or guidance, follow up and let them know how you used that advice and make it clear that you were listening and executed thoughtful actions from their imparted wisdom. These actions go much further in building social capital than most people realize and can easily be accomplished by using calendar reminders or an online task list.

3. **Pay it forward:** If you make an introduction for someone in your network that leads to anything valuable for either person, your social capital account with both people increases (as Bill's account increased with John BoardMember and my own). Channeling JFK, I advise you to ask what you can do for your network *before* asking what your network can do for you. Whether you are looking to get a job, sell something, partner with a business, or hire the right team member, it's helpful to have already built up social capital before you need to go to the well. This is an especially smart move for people who have strong, high-quality networks but who wonder how they can monetize that social capital (or get a job) through their networks without abusing them. If you fall into this category, the following is a painless process worth considering:

a. First, find an ethical, well-connected person in your network with whom you like spending time.

b. Determine what this person—we'll call her Jane Awesome—is trying to achieve at this point in her life. You can do so by simply taking her out to lunch and asking her what she's up to. Learning about Awesome's goals and figuring out her value proposition and target market will better arm you to make a quality introduction for her from the pool of people you know.

c. Make an unsolicited and thoughtful introduction. This act may turn into a business deal, an achieved goal, or just a new connection for Awesome. Offering some form of positive result (even if it is nothing significant) puts Awesome in an appreciative position, which will allow you to be more comfortable asking her for an introduction to someone in *her* network when you need one later on. Not only are you positioning yourself well for future tangible gain, but you've also helped your friend.

Note: Please do not mistake my words (here or anywhere else in this book) for saying that you should be nice to people and make introductions *just so* you can take advantage of that relationship later. The people in your network will notice if you are insincere, which will prevent you from building social capital stores with anyone. This tip (and any others I provide) is merely an explanation of how to do something that *could* help you build social capital in the future; it does not guarantee it. That absence of the guarantee is actually what makes it so valuable. People appreciate what you do more if you choose to help them because you like them instead of because you are *expecting* a return on that investment of your time and brand.

4. **Grab a coffee and hang out by a crosswalk:** Let's just say that if, one day, you happen to see a man walking, distracted while deep in thought, and he fails to notice he is about to step into a crosswalk while traffic has not yet slowed, and you grab his arm and save his life . . . you'll most likely be able to ask him for an

introduction or two. Perhaps this scenario is far-fetched; however, it does highlight the point that sometimes it's not the length of a relationship that matters in generating social capital but the *quality* of that time spent.

Carrying the Pig and Talking to Trees

A valuable lesson I learned in the realm of social capital best practices occurred when I was a student in Fort Benning's U.S. Army Ranger School—a rigorous leadership and educational experience that challenges physical, intellectual, and *social* capabilities, requiring the highest degree of attention to detail and mental focus. Ranger School consists of three phases covering at least 63 days. You must pass many levels of evaluation to earn the right to call yourself Ranger. The basic evaluative tool during this experience is the patrol; you essentially live in the woods with your squad or platoon, executing full-day—as in 24-hour-long—missions. There is an assigned (and graded) patrol leader, with subordinate (also graded) leadership roles, all of which rotate twice *during* each mission. This process requires that you pay meticulous attention to other people's duties so that you can then lead effectively in your next position, since you're not told until the moment you are promoted what your role will be for the next iteration. Therefore, you don't get through Ranger School without building some strong ties to your fellow students whom you've likely just met only days or weeks before.

A unique element of Ranger School that can jeopardize a stellar patrol assessment is the peer review. You can be "peered out," which can cause you to fail out of Ranger School, even if you demonstrate the tactical genius of General Patton and the physical stamina of a samurai while passing your patrols with flying colors. If your peers decide that they don't like you (and they don't even need to provide hard evidence of it), you will never be able to call yourself a Ranger.

I realized very early on during Ranger School that I would build social capital most effectively by discovering how to use my strengths to help the people around me *without* asking for anything in return. It quickly became apparent that the only effective way to be seen as a good guy here was to actually *be* a good guy. Extremely stressful situations tend to cause people to drop their guard and let their true colors show through.

Since I came from the armor branch, not the infantry, I was at a disadvantage when I arrived at Fort Benning; my core training up to that point wasn't as focused on Ranger School's infantry-focused tactics as was many of my peers'. Therefore, lending tactical genius was *not* how I intended to build social capital. However, after almost a year of intense preparatory training, I quickly realized that at a lean 205 pounds, my physical strength was an asset I could use to be a good team member. I would regularly volunteer to carry the heavier gear during the patrols and road marches we conducted early on, specifically the 24-pound M60 machine gun affectionately referred to as the *Pig*.

Few people *wanted* to carry the Pig (in addition to another 40 to 80 pounds of gear that we all had already), but because I was willing to use any advantage I had in size to benefit my peers, I offered to do so more often than not. And I never complained, making sure always to look at the silver lining of tough situations and remain upbeat. I took the same stance when a peer in a leadership position would ask me to complete an unpleasant task: I executed the task to the best of my ability and kept any grumblings to myself.

My social capital payday manifested itself during the second part of Ranger School: the mountain phase. One dark night during a graded patrol, I came down with a sickness I later realized was probably the flu. I had a fever, became delirious, and most notably, lost my appetite (the significance of the

(continued)

(*continued*)

latter symptom highlights the severity of my illness as every other day in Ranger School, I would have likely traded a kidney for a candy bar).

Needless to say, I was *not* a functional Ranger while my head was on the chopping block as an evaluated patrol leader. Because of the strong desire to avoid being recycled, I powered through my initial duties while drinking as much water as I could, trying to purge my system of this ill-timed curse. My final requirement for that patrol was to complete a long march at night, carrying a heavy load through mountainous terrain. I was so sick, malnourished, and tired that I was later told I was falling in and out of consciousness, talking aimlessly to the surrounding forest. My buddies could tell I was having a difficult time, but because of the social capital I'd built up with them from taking on Pig duty and being a good team player, they jumped in to help me. Although it would have been easier for my peers to leave me behind or to tell an RI (Ranger Instructor) that I was sick, they instead tied a strap to my rifle and led me through the mountains so I wouldn't get lost. It was because of my fellow Rangers that I made it through the night. Had I not built social capital with these people beforehand, I may never have earned my Ranger Tab, which would make this story far less interesting.

And for good measure, consider the following few worst practices:

1. **Don't milk your introductions:** I was once introduced to a new business partner by someone we'll call John Milker. Milker's self-interest prompted him to promote his own agenda by keeping himself involved in the relationship he stimulated, despite there being no mutually beneficial reason to do so. He continued to entangle himself in the new relationship as things

progressed and it became awkward when all the other parties realized he didn't fit. However, since Milker made the introduction, it was a difficult topic to bring up. His selfish mentality rapidly burned social capital with me and our mutual business partner, and it was clearly not worth his effort to force his involvement.

2. **Don't treat people as a means to an end:** People generally know when someone else has used or is using them. Treat people like the friends, contacts, and respected employees they are while you network, and not like tools that you're trying to manipulate. As I reiterate throughout the book—this is not to say that you should *only* be nice to people you will want something from in the future. We all know someone who operates under this mentality, and it is usually transparent and not appreciated.

3. **Don't try to cash in on social capital:** I was once introduced to a potential business partner by someone I'll refer to as John Greedy. When the introduction turned to business, Greedy ended up coming back and saying, "By the way, since I introduced you, I want a cut of whatever comes out of it." Although his request was based on the general notion of the commonly accepted practice for referral revenue sharing, the fact that he hadn't clarified this up front soured the relationship. If you make an introduction for someone without clearly outlining some form of agreement before doing so, be careful. You can burn stores of social capital by pursuing monetary compensation after the fact.

4. **Don't make flippant introductions:** This is where using Linked-In became confusing for many early adopters who lost sight of their objective in pursuit of sincere intentions. Some believe that introductions are a quantity-based activity instead of a quality-based one, and thereby they make introductions solely for the sake of introducing people. Despite having access to a plethora of people you never knew you could reach, you never want to waste your connections' time by being a super-introducer who doesn't carefully consider whether or not *both* sides of the equation will benefit from the interaction.

Second Lieutenant AllTalk and the Tab Wearers

I also learned a couple of social capital worst practices in my time at Fort Benning. Unfortunately, there are some people who believe they can glide through Ranger School (and life) by relying exclusively on social capital. Take for example, Second Lieutenant AllTalk. AllTalk entered Ranger School, the Army's preeminent leadership school using infantry tactics as the educational medium, as a noninfantry officer with even less tactical preparation than I had under my belt. AllTalk arrived thinking he was just going to do favors for people to make them like him, and he didn't think he needed to learn the infantry tactics that were required to excel. AllTalk believed that his infantry friends would take care of him when it was his turn to lead patrols, because he was generating a lot of social capital for them (for example, sharing his food with them and volunteering to take the lead on miserable or laborious tasks). But the Ranger Instructors could tell that he wasn't proficient in his duties. This was partly due to the fact that his peers realized that AllTalk *expected* to lean on them while they were tired, hungry, and cold as well. AllTalk wasn't able to pass his patrols because he relied too much on social capital; he didn't earn the title of Ranger, because he was depending on others to carry his load. He didn't *get* social capital, and he didn't get his tab either.

Had AllTalk managed to slide by and become a Ranger, he probably would have been what the Army calls a "tab *wearer*"— people who attend Ranger School solely to get their tabs and then rest on their laurels afterward. They simply show their prize off to everyone in a "Hey, look at me!" fashion. On the other hand, if you're a "tab *bearer*," you recognize that because you've earned that tab, it's now your duty to represent it well. You show that you deserve it by being an ambassador for the Ranger brand as opposed to milking it. When this concept is applied to social capital, you become a tab wearer when you use someone as a means to achieve an end and then treat them as something from your past. Conversely, you become a social capital tab bearer when you recognize that it takes work to maintain a relationship, which includes providing meaningful introductions and other means of returning value to people who have helped you, because it's the right thing to do. Being a tab bearer means that you always keep that delicate balance that is the social capital exchange in mind.

You generally won't build social capital by poking prospective business partners on Facebook or tweeting them on Twitter. That's not to say that these forms of social media are not effective business tools. I just want to stress that social capital is not as effectively exchanged in other platforms deemed "social," as LinkedIn is the best of the breed in this arena. Another way to see this is that Facebook answers the question, "what are my friends doing right now?" while LinkedIn answers the question, "who in my network can introduce me to someone I need to meet?" LinkedIn is fundamentally different from any other site that has been categorized as social media. And on that note, it's about time we discuss the star of the show. . . .

Chapter 1 Summary

- Unlike financial capital, social capital cannot be bought. It takes time and trust to earn, maintain, and use (not abuse) social capital. But it is the building up, cashing in, and exchanging of social capital that molds and powers the world of business today.
- I define social capital as the intangible value Person A assigns to Person B when Person B asks for some type of favor from Person A (an introduction, a recommendation, provision of business intelligence, and so on).
- LinkedIn enhances some antiquated ways of spreading word of mouth (WOM) marketing and provides, for the first time ever, the ability for users to directly stimulate personal WOM marketing to multiple target markets.

2

LinkedIn-a-Nutshell

SOCIAL MEDIA HAS drastically and irreversibly altered the way we communicate with each other, gather information, and conduct business in this new era. In many ways, it is positively transforming our society. However, when it comes to LinkedIn, the term *social media* just doesn't apply, and here's why: the term *social media* suggests a social interaction and communication between users. Ironically, for professionals who target professionals, it's not the *social* part that doesn't work (I will discuss the power of social network analysis in the context of professional relationships later). Rather, it's the *media* piece that doesn't accurately describe LinkedIn's highest value proposition.

Webster's online dictionary provides this excerpt on the word *media*: "in references to the agencies of mass communication. . . ."[1]

Unlike media, LinkedIn's *power* for professionals is not based on mass communication (such as advertising, PR, and Twitter campaigning). It's based on a *mass utilization* of your current relationships to comfortably stimulate new ones.

Since I've mentioned already that I believe LinkedIn to be ahead of its time, I'll explain how I see the world currently using LinkedIn with a bit of historical fiction. Let's say a secret division at Apple miscalculated during the tests of a new time-travel iPhone application. This mishap results in a box filled with 10 of the most cutting-edge iPhones being sent back in time 20,000 years, just steps in front of John FossilFriend's morning stroll with his pet mastodon.

What would happen? FossilFriend would look at the box, take a bite out of one of the phones, and in finding little value or taste, he'd probably just take the box home to his family to see if they could find some use for the new objects. Let's then assume that FossilFriend's buddy, John LightningRod, invents fire a few weeks later. LightningRod's discovery would show the cave world the value of fire, which includes the value of light. When baby FossilFriend happens to be playing in the box of iPhones one day and accidentally stumbles upon the "on" button, a new value is realized: portable light. Thus, FossilFriend leads his family around the tar pits, holding his iTorch in the air with heroic pride, despite the tremendous value that lies just a bit deeper beyond "on."

So let's fast-forward to present day to see a similar scenario. LinkedIn came our way in 2003. A year later, Facebook joined our world and took center stage in front of the preexisting social websites, since it was flashier, more exciting, and more useful for social purposes. Then when LinkedIn reached its critical mass of users, those using it still categorized it into what they thought it to be: social media, while a much greater value quietly emerged behind the same LinkedIn logo.

The Proof Is in the Peacock

I was recently put in touch with a highly regarded advertising executive we'll call John Peacock—someone who's programmed to think in terms of the mass communications that Webster described above. I was introduced to him under my *Boston Globe*-provided title, LinkedIn Jedi. Early in our introductory and only call, Peacock mentioned, with a tone of defensive assertion: "You know, I can see that you looked at my

LinkedIn Profile, but you can't tell that I looked at yours, because I know how to turn that feature off." Seven seconds later, I learned that Peacock considered himself to be a LinkedIn expert, and it appeared he felt the need to prove something to me. This first impression with Peacock kept me from seeking a second call for several reasons:

1. Peacock thought I didn't know how to go into what I call *stealth mode* when viewing others' Profiles because I looked at his Profile and he saw my full name and headline in the "Who's Viewed My Profile" section. However, because he saw my full information prior to our call and the only way he could have seen that is if I manually selected it, his credibility as an expert on the topic was questionable.

2. He considered himself a LinkedIn expert, and he chose a very basic feature to mention as one that he felt differentiated his abilities from other self-proclaimed LinkedIn illuminati.

3. He was a fast-talker who liked to control the conversation (just as some unenlightened executives attempt to do the same in regard to their clients' messaging, instead of *listening* to what is being said to or about them). Yet when I asked him how he used his automated searches, he fell silent. He then said, "Well, I'm not exactly sure what you mean by that, but I'm certain our team knows every way there is in LinkedIn to *reach the maximum number of people* in our clients' target markets." Call up the mental image of prehistoric-Peacock holding his iTorch high in the air. . . .

4. He was somewhat *combative*. He tried to dominate the call and spoke arrogantly about his LinkedIn skills even though I was introduced to him by one of his longtime trusted friends, John BadIntro. Notably, I met BadIntro when he saw me speak at a conference just a few weeks

(continued)

(*continued*)

prior to this call. Although I didn't know BadIntro well, I took this call because he was a senior executive at an impressive firm. I made a judgment call about BadIntro and the type of professional he would introduce me to, and I was wrong.

So instead of a pleasant interaction, Peacock provided an example of how one successful, well-respected executive in the field of advertising (also known as *mass communication*) views LinkedIn. It also demonstrates the double-edged sword that introductions can be, if not made with thoughtfulness . . . as you can imagine BadIntro didn't earn any social capital with me because of this introduction.

Untapped Resources

Going beyond semantics, the difference between Facebook and LinkedIn isn't fully explained by the common phrase, "LinkedIn's for business, and Facebook's for fun." There's another fundamental distinction between LinkedIn and any social media site—one nested in the information that you can get from LinkedIn that you cannot get anywhere else in the world. LinkedIn's mission is "to connect the world's professionals to make them more productive and successful. [The company and its employees believe that] in a global connected economy, your success as a professional and your competitiveness as a company depend upon faster access to insight and resources you can trust."[2] And LinkedIn, more than any other tool, is uniquely positioned to achieve this goal.

In December 2009, the *Wall Street Journal* predicted that LinkedIn would lose out to Facebook if it didn't get its users to engage and spend more time on the website.[3] This supports the claim that many tech-savvy members of the media (and in particular, this highly respected, popular source) grouped LinkedIn with other sites under the category of social media. The article also reflects much of the initial opposition we first received from our clients when telling them that we focused on LinkedIn: at the time, Facebook users visited the site 10 times a day, and LinkedIn users only averaged about four visits per week.

What those people didn't grasp is that LinkedIn's value to its users is not found in the mass projection or sustained online inter-action capabilities that social media sites like Facebook boast. LinkedIn isn't about how much time you spend on it; it's about how *well* you spend that time. A surgeon doesn't need to use a scal-pel for a long period of time to save a life; she just needs to use it in a precise and methodical way. LinkedIn is that scalpel.

LinkedIn does not directly compete with Facebook in this context because it provides different tools for different audiences. Users should consider LinkedIn to be a business intelligence tool and use it as such. If the surgeon I just mentioned goes into an operating room to save a life, having built up her knowledge of surgical practice and how to use that scalpel, she is postured to accomplish her goal. If she stands over her patient and is handed a butter knife by her nurse—well, you'll probably see that nurse using LinkedIn's job search features soon afterward.

Now, *I* may walk into that operating room, see the scalpel and the butter knife, and because of my ignorance of surgical practices, say that they could *probably* be used for the same purpose in the hands of a master surgeon. From a distance and to the untrained eye, they're similar, right? But much like social media (or tools mistaken for social media, like LinkedIn), being too far removed from them and inexperienced with them has led to mass confusion and misuse.

So here I am, a LinkedIn surgeon, watching people compare the scalpel (LinkedIn) to the butter knife (Facebook, Myspace, and so forth), urging the world to wake up from its social techno-logy slumber to use LinkedIn the right way.

Further differentiating these online tools is the distinct value that each produces. To illustrate this point, when I just *googled* "Steve Vinter" (who happens to be a RockTech Advisory Board Member and who also runs Google's office in Cambridge), the first search result that currently appears is his LinkedIn Profile, notably above his Twitter and Facebook pages. And although LinkedIn now has a fraction of the users of Facebook with less user activity than Twitter, Google selects what it perceives as *valuable* to rank order search results. I've often heard LinkedIn executives reference each of their users' Profiles as the "public profile of record," or the standard for displaying your professional identify online. It appears LinkedIn has achieved this status, and Google agrees.

SEO Value: Googling a Google Guy

Search engine optimization (SEO) is a practice that allows people and companies to compete with others to rank their websites as high as they can in organic search engine results for specific keywords or phrases. SEO is part art and part science, because the algorithm used to determine which websites earn the top spots, based on keyword searches, isn't made public and is designed not to be reverse engineered. If the secret sauce of SEO were made public by Google, Yahoo!, Bing, or other search engines, technical gurus would find a way to cheat and ensure that their websites rank high. Search results would then be based on technical savvy instead of the true value delivered by the web page.

Therefore, since we can't provide mathematical proof of LinkedIn's SEO value, we can only judge it based on the competitive results we see when we conduct searches. If you *google* someone who puts time into creating a quality LinkedIn Profile, that's probably what you're going to see first: the LinkedIn Profile they personally authored and want the world to see about them. There are many companies found on the Internet trying to sell your information in the form of e-mail lists, cold call lists, and mailing lists. You would likely agree that when someone searches for you, it's preferable to have what *you* say about yourself rank as the top result versus the unapproved information about you that companies are trying to sell.

I don't have the SEO prowess to tell you exactly how LinkedIn surpasses competitors in Google searches, but I know the guy who can: former Google executive Deep Nishar, who happens to be

LinkedIn's current senior vice president of Products & User Experience. With one look at the impressive credentials in his LinkedIn Profile, you can tell that Deep's leadership is a huge asset to LinkedIn's value. I was introduced to Deep in 2009 by Jeff Glass, one of LinkedIn's investors from Bain Capital Ventures. After Jeff had led a $53 million investment round in LinkedIn,[4] he introduced me to Deep in an e-mail including this comment:

> "Dave, Deep is a product and business guru. Someday after LinkedIn goes public for zillions and Deep decides to start another company, I will write him a check without needing to even hear the idea. I only hope he deposits my check!"

As someone who held a high level position at Google and has earned this level of respect from his investors, Deep is the cerebral cortex powering LinkedIn's SEO.

The Object of Our Affection

LinkedIn's impressive background is yet another means of distinguishing it from other social media. The company was first conceived in 2002 in the same way that many other good ideas are: in someone's living room. Reid Hoffman, LinkedIn's principal cofounder, understood and wanted to capitalize on the value of business relationships (hence LinkedIn's motto: *Relationships Matter*), and he chose to create technology that would activate this value for professionals around the world. Reid has since stated, "LinkedIn had something to do with how I think the Internet works, how it changes people's lives." The website officially launched on May 5, 2003, and set out to change people's lives with only about 350 contacts, who were invited by the founding team. At the end of the month, LinkedIn was up to 4,500 members, reaching the half-million user mark in April 2004. Three years later, LinkedIn's number was at 10 million. In early 2011, it crossed the milestone threshold of 100 million users worldwide.

Since "Cinco de LinkedIn" (the company employees' affectionate name for the launch date), the site also gained financial backing from investors including Sequoia, Greylock, Bain Capital Ventures, Bessemer, European Founders, Goldman Sachs, McGraw-Hill Companies, and SAP Ventures. Over the years, LinkedIn has enhanced its services by launching many additional features such as LinkedIn Jobs, Answers, Applications, Polls, and the Grad Guide, to name a few. It has partnered with the *New York Times*, CNBC, Amazon, Google, Wordpress, TripIt, Twitter, and many others to create integrated applications. And as of May 19, 2011, LinkedIn became a publicly traded company and finished the day with a stock price valuing it at nearly $9 billion.[5]

With the many new features and facets of LinkedIn, Reid Hoffman still managed to sum up the site pretty simply when he said, "Everyone's a publisher, everyone has identity, and these trusted networks are going to be the things that filter signal from noise."[6]

Taming the LIONs

However, compared to today, that's just what LinkedIn was in the beginning: a bunch of noise. Many of the more vocal initial users included sales professionals trying to reach as many customers as they could and recruiters seeking contact with as many job searchers as possible. We refer to these overzealous, early users as super-connectors—people who connected with anyone and everyone. Instead of accurately and intentionally mapping their true networks, these people were simply trying to connect with as many individuals as possible, whether they knew them or not. This behavior is based on a basic and widely accepted mathematical business theory: the more leads or candidates to whom you gain access, the higher the probability you'll close a deal or get a placement—right?

I don't think so, and neither did LinkedIn, whose leaders developed measures to discourage super-connecting in order to protect its user ecosystem's fidelity. Super-connecting still occurs with the endangered species of people who refer to themselves as

LIONs—LinkedIn Open Networkers. Users who connect with LIONs can be confident that they won't be turned down when sending said LION an invitation to connect.

I highlight these early super-connectors and LIONs because the way that they use LinkedIn defeats the site's fundamental value and most important aspect, and this usage was what discouraged some professionals from joining or using LinkedIn afterward. LinkedIn utilizes its patented six degrees of separation technology[7] to provide us with the ability to see who we know and who we can get warmly introduced to *through* the people we know. I suspect most of you will agree that one of your most precious assets is your real-world network of trusted contacts (which LinkedIn defines as including your 1st, 2nd, and 3rd degree connections). Yet, unless you use LinkedIn correctly, you can't gain a true understanding of the real current value of this asset. Hints of this value are seen every time someone you know introduces you to someone you *want* to know. Imagine the increase in value your network would provide you if you didn't have to wait for these introductions, but could just ask for them today.

Users who map their actual networks via LinkedIn can clearly see the relationship paths to other users. If everyone simply connected to everyone, LinkedIn's value would be nothing more than FossilFriend's iTorch. You would have an incorrectly mapped network, filled with people you don't actually know—people for or to whom you couldn't make a warm introduction.

So how do you start mapping *your* network? Well, there's the hard way, and there's the smart way.

Chapter 2 Summary

- LinkedIn is more of a social business intelligence tool than it is social media because *media* indicates mass projection of communications, which is not how LinkedIn is most effective for professionals.
- A fundamental distinction between LinkedIn and any social media site lies within the relationship information you can get

from LinkedIn that you cannot get anywhere else in online or offline sources.

- LinkedIn LIONs and super-connectors have influenced sub-groups of the general public to dilute their networks by overconnecting. This common behavior will misguide them from the course that will allow LinkedIn to function at its highest utility.

3

Social Network Analysis

WHEN SPEAKING TO groups about LinkedIn, I often ask a brave member of the audience to define the word *network*. Normally, the first answer I get is, "The people we know." Then some guy in the back, who thinks he knows what I'm going to say, suggests, "It's the people we know *and trust*."

I appreciate the enthusiasm and contributions; so if you heard me speak at a conference or other event, gave a response, and are now reading this book, I thank you. But as many thousands of conference attendees now know, it's not that simple. There is actually a much more scientific and valuable definition for our *network* and the analysis surrounding it. As a graduate student, I took a course on social networks that opened my eyes to the true meaning of this commonly misused term and how to map it.

Mapping Your Real Network

The actual map of our network extends far beyond the people we know and trust—people who *should* be our 1st degree connections in LinkedIn. It is actually our 2nd and 3rd degree connections that populate the majority of our real network maps—a number of people that is exponentially greater than just our 1st degree connections. These people have always existed around us, but timely access to them has never been available . . . prior to LinkedIn. In *Social Network Analysis: Methods and Applications (Structural Analysis in the Social Sciences)*, Katherine Faust and Stanley Wasserman state that in the context of our actual social network map, "Relational ties (linkages) between actors are channels for transfer or 'flow' of resources."

Why should you care about this? Well, if you always thought your network included only the people you know or have known, then you have experienced an exponentially lower "flow" of resources available to you than what actually exists. When you use LinkedIn to map your actual network, you have access to those 2nd and 3rd degree connections, removing the metaphorical dam from that greater "flow" of resources. These resources often tangibly manifest themselves as introductions for job offers, sales leads, expertise requests, or other forms of social business intelligence. Your network map is a measurable depiction of your active (and more importantly, *potentially* active) relationships. And LinkedIn can activate those relationships for you.

The world's overuse and resultant dilution of the phrase *social networking* has confused the meaning for many people who attempt to leverage social technologies such as LinkedIn. Now that discussions of network theory have moved outside the classroom and into the boardroom, professionals strive to understand and integrate its power into their businesses. However, not many appreciate that achieving useful power in this realm begins with the ability to effectively map dynamic personal networks.

What does all of this have to do with LinkedIn? Jens Krause et al. teed it up nicely when they stated in "Social network theory in the behavioural sciences: potential applications" that "Networks tell us who is connected to whom in the population and by what relationship. An individual's network position (that is, its social environment) may also have important . . . consequences."[1] That has LinkedIn written all over it.

To help you to visually understand the aforementioned academic literature, I've provided a couple of examples. When drawn out, a (very small) personal network may look like Figure 3.1.

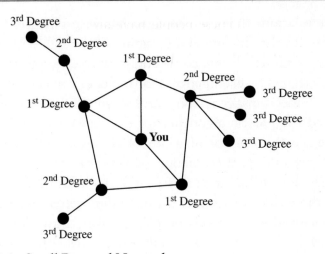

Figure 3.1   Small Personal Network

Each black circle represents an individual, also known as a node. The lines that connect the nodes (called links) symbolize the relationship between any two individuals.

Instead of the image in Figure 3.1, your network likely looks something like mine. To see this more clearly, my 1st degree network is demonstrated by the LinkedIn InMap tool shown in Figure 3.2. One of LinkedIn's visual network mapping tools, this InMap graphically represents my network of 1st degree connections and

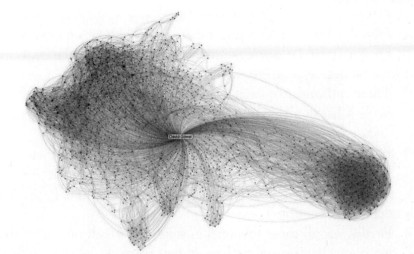

Figure 3.2   My Network Charted by LinkedIn InMap

the interrelations that each of them has with one another. The sensitivity in the shading and grouping of the different nodes in this map of my 1st degree connections represents a form of commonality shared by each person that includes companies, schools, mutual connections, geography, and so on (LinkedIn has not yet published the precise algorithm for this tool). Recognizing that you can see the interior relations of all these individual nodes through my InMap, think about the fact that each one of these nodes has its own InMap of all its 1st degree relationships in addition to those shared with me. If this InMap were to reflect reality and be mapped to accurately portray everyone I know and everyone they know, this image would cover the entire market of clients, employees, service providers, and so on that I may want to know—meaning I can get to them through a warm introduction or word of mouth. (Go to http://inmaps.linkedinlabs.com/ to map your own network.)

Fortunately, none of us must comprehend the broad-reaching depths of network theory to understand, and more importantly use, the power of the basic concept behind LinkedIn. Yet, while people have been loosely using the term *social network* for years, we haven't been able to truly map out and use these network linkages until now. Why not? Well, here's what it would take to manually map out your actual network:

1. Start by listing every single person you know or have ever known (your 1st degree connections—again, for clarity, only my 1st degree connections are shown in Figure 3.2).
2. Then call and ask each of those 1st degree connections to make a list of all their 1st degree connections (these are your 2nd degree connections).
3. Before you hang up the phone, ask your 1st degree connections to then call everyone on that list from step two to ask *them* to make a list of each of *their* 1st degree connections (your 3rd degree connections).
4. Finally, ask all those involved in steps 1–3 to inform you of the real-time changes to their lists as their networks grow over time.

Your Network of Trusted Professionals

You are at the center of your network. Your connections can introduce you to 10,829,400+ professionals — here's how your network breaks down:

1	**Your Connections** Your trusted friends and colleagues	1,481
2	**Two degrees away** Friends of friends; each connected to one of your connections	437,100+
3	**Three degrees away** Reach these users through a friend and one of their friends	10,390,800+
	Total users you can contact through an Introduction	10,829,400+

Figure 3.3   LinkedIn Network Statistics

The impracticality of this activity makes it clear why the information that LinkedIn provides has never been available and how it is also tremendously significant. Previously, only upon completion of these tasks would you have access to understand the first three degrees of your network. This begs the question: In the past, what did *you* actually mean when you referred to your *network*?

LinkedIn's definition of network includes your 1st, 2nd, and 3rd degree connections, which, according to LinkedIn's Network Statistics feature, means that my current network comprises nearly 11 million people, as shown in Figure 3.3.

For the first time in history, we are able to tangibly view and more fully utilize these networks—thanks to LinkedIn. You can visibly map the path that will lead you to the target person of that company you've been trying to reach. Oh, and that currently unknown *path*? It may be just one short step, perhaps in the form of a phone call to your current neighbor or college roommate.

The interesting point to consider is that although your network wasn't always easily available to you, it has always existed. John OldFriend may have known Jane TargetMarket for 10 years. Even though OldFriend is a pal, you're not about to ask him to list *every single one* of his acquaintances to see if he has people in his circle of friends who fit your target market. And because his connection to TargetMarket never came up in your usual conversations, you've been in the dark and would otherwise remain there in terms of knowing about their relationship. Do you think all the people you know have deliberately learned all the value propositions for you and everyone else they know, to be sure they are making relevant introductions when they can? Have *you* done this for everyone you know? Probably not. Therefore, you are likely just one phone call away from someone who can change your life or your business; you just don't know it yet.

Connecting to the 3rd Degree

Although many people are wary of reaching out to 3rd degree connections on LinkedIn, most are comfortable with the concept of tactfully asking for an introduction from someone whom they know well. But the idea of having a contact introduce you to someone, who will *then* introduce you to someone else, can seem a bit daunting. Could this series of meetings possibly be worth the effort? My first significant foray into using this feature illustrates one of many opportunities available by leveraging 3rd degree connections.

It was in 2008 when my marketing firm collaborated with a nonprofit organization in the Boston suburb where I lived to put on an unprecedented event for the local business community, which we'll call BigEvent. BigEvent was tailored to local small businesses and entrepreneurs in an effort to provide practical e-marketing techniques from industry experts on various topics including e-mail marketing, SEO, social media, and online advertising. Throughout the time we planned BigEvent, I was still running my company with my wife out of our back porch on nights and weekends while teaching ROTC at MIT. I didn't have the network (or the time) I have today to ensure our portion of the responsibilities for this event's success.

Jane NonProfitExec, who was the head of the nonprofit organization running this event, informed me that one large local company would be the perfect sponsor for the event; we'll call them SponsorUs, Inc. Inconveniently, her point of contact at SponsorUs, John GateKeeper, had decided our event wasn't a good fit for them at that time. One of NonProfitExec's most admirable traits is her determination; as such, she was undeterred by GateKeeper's response and openly pondered in my presence, "If only there were a way we could get to GateKeeper's boss, Jane DecideStuff, because *she* would see the value of our event."

Already a LinkedIn zealot at the time, I knew what to do. I performed a simple search and quickly found that Decide-Stuff was in fact a 3rd degree connection of mine. My 1st degree connection linking me to her was John FirstDegree, a well-connected friend, who worked for one of our clients. I put in a call to John to ask him who he knew who also knew DecideStuff. I was informed that his mutual connection to her was Basil Harris Jr. When I asked John, "How well do you know Basil? Is he someone you think I would get along with?" he replied, "Dave, not only is Basil a good guy whom I know well, but I'm sure you two will get along."

John exchanged some social capital for me by sending Basil a note asking if he'd be willing to talk to me about a potential DecideStuff introduction. Basil agreed via e-mail, and we set up a call to discuss it further. After talking to Basil for less than an hour, he too agreed that I would be a good fit for this introduction, and said that he'd love to put us together to see what would come of it. I received a very warm introduction from Basil, and I met with DecideStuff for coffee less than 10 days after NonProfitExec had made the simple comment, "If only there were a way . . . ."

At our java rendezvous, DecideStuff and I started discussing our respective businesses. I explained what BigEvent was and why we were doing it. Before I half-consumed my choco-croissant, she asked if we were looking for sponsors and appeared to be hooked on the idea. Eager to get involved, she

(continued)

(*continued*)

said, "Let me talk to my team member who handles this for me, John GateKeeper; I'm sure he'd *love* to make this happen." Two days later, NonProfitExec received a call from GateKeeper saying that he had reconsidered and would love to sponsor our event.

The remarkable point here is that I never would have been able to ask for this introduction without LinkedIn. I could have searched via Google for DecideStuff, but no other tools existed that could have revealed that path of my relationships that would lead me to her.

Considering the steps that occurred to make that network path available for me to see, several important things went on behind the scenes on LinkedIn's servers. If I hadn't connected via LinkedIn to John, who then hadn't connected to Basil, who then hadn't connected to DecideStuff (or even if just one of those was a missing link), this whole opportunity for this introduction would not have been possible. This is why it is helpful for you to connect to *all* the people whom you know and encourage everyone in your network to also mirror their real-world networks on LinkedIn.

BigEvent worked out tremendously well for everyone involved. After the event, I was invited by SponsorUs to present on LinkedIn for about 40 senior executives, representing SponsorUs's clients at their headquarters. I was then featured on SponsorUs's webinar circuit which, at the time, was being viewed by about 60,000 people per year. Furthermore, if you look at Basil Harris Jr.'s LinkedIn Profile, you'll notice Clearly Creative on there, as I ultimately hired him. That relationship all started with me performing a LinkedIn search for a person to whom I wanted to get introduced. This was a noteworthy success and a glimpse of the power of your network when it is well-mapped in LinkedIn, including those "useless" 3rd degree connections.

It's Not Just What You Know

Here's a bold statement for you: LinkedIn's search capabilities are going to be more valuable than Google's search capabilities. I'm not just saying this to get your attention, and I don't even see LinkedIn as a competitor of Google, but the fact that they both provide search capabilities is worth discussion. Consider first that Google search does not primarily *create* information; it provides a phenomenal resource to *access* it. The data Google provides via its search capabilities were previously available in sources such as phone books, scholarly journals, library archives, restaurant menus, and newspapers. Google has just dominated the market share in organizing and expediting our access to the world's information stores.

On the other hand, LinkedIn's information about the links within your network has always existed. Yet no matter how long you searched, you could never easily explore the details of your 1st degree, 2nd degree, and 3rd degree network members. If you had to try, the process would be as dauntingly time-consuming as I described in the previous section (calling everyone you know, to call everyone they know, to call everyone they know, and so on). While this method is unrealistic, most who grasp its power will tell you that the information it would yield is unparalleled—valuable to the point where it's *almost* worth it to pick up the phone and start dialing. But don't invest in multiple phone lines and highly caffeinated beverages just yet.

LinkedIn provides you this information that you cannot get *anywhere else in the world*, which is why it is bringing unprecedented value to business as we know it, even if you choose not to upgrade to its premium offerings.[2]

This technology is redefining how people network, how professionals find and gain business intelligence, and how the world does business in general. This fact hit me soon after I started my major career shift from military to civilian life. I determined that LinkedIn isn't social media; it truly is a *game-changing* business tool. Consequently, I dove headfirst into discovering just how to make it work for me and eventually for my clients. Consulting on

LinkedIn became our most popular service, which was an initial step on my path to RockTech. Chapter 4 describes what many of our clients since 2007 have found to be the most valuable feature of LinkedIn, which, when used properly, will show you how LinkedIn is fundamentally changing the nature of how professionals interact.

Chapter 3 Summary

- Your network is an accurate and measurable depiction of active (and, more importantly, potentially active) relationships. It includes the people you know as well as the people you can efficiently access *through* the people you know.
- The world's dilution of the phrase *social networking* has confused the meaning for most people who sit in front of a computer to leverage social technologies such as LinkedIn.
- Although your personal network has always existed, manually drawing this network has been impossible for most, making the information that LinkedIn provides incredibly significant. For the first time in history, we are able to tangibly view and more fully utilize our networks by using LinkedIn.
- LinkedIn's search capabilities are valuable because they provide access to unprecedented and self-updating relationship information.

4

A Search That Is Truly Advanced

I ONCE HAD a conversation with a c-level executive in a publicly traded company—I'll call him John WantItNow—who asked me to list my "top five" best tips and tricks for using LinkedIn. WantItNow was hoping to receive some quick, "flashy" nuggets of wisdom that he could take back to his company, thereby immediately demonstrating the value of the tool to his leaders, managers, and employees. Like many people, WantItNow didn't see that the strategic value of LinkedIn requires an ongoing methodology to understand. He assumed that a "short and sweet" list of five tips would enable his corporation to wake up to LinkedIn's power.

Giving WantItNow the list he requested to bring back to his company would be similar to giving a new driver a list of top five tips on how to drive that shiny new car he received for his birthday—and then tossing him the keys. The inexperienced driver wants to get on the road and start driving immediately, despite not yet having the skills to effectively do so. Likely, he would get behind the wheel and stay on the cautious side . . . at first. Then a false sense of security may lead him to *feel* like he knows the rules of the road, causing him to head for the highway when he's not quite ready to leave the parking lot. This approach—both with driving and with LinkedIn—is not likely to lead to a desired outcome.

In both scenarios, my actual "top five" lists would be useful, but they're not going to make anyone jump out of their seat with excitement. For a new driver—the list would probably include checking the tire pressure, fluids, turn signals, brakes, and planning the route. For someone looking to adopt LinkedIn, it is also good to start with a similar list—boring but important—focusing first on setting up privacy considerations. I wouldn't begin by showing WantItNow how to use LinkedIn's unprecedented business tools, just as a driving instructor wouldn't start a lesson with the new driver by showing him how to switch lanes on a busy highway. Had I given that lackluster list to WantItNow, it likely would not have been compelling enough for his company to see the business value in LinkedIn. But it *is* where they should be starting.

My intention here is to explain why sending the short and sweet list that WantItNow originally requested would strategically be a bad move. Just as a new driver is likely to veer off course without the proper guidance and practice, each employee would be risking their personal and corporate brands when they attempt to execute this list without adopting the ongoing methodology that LinkedIn requires. A wrong turn could be disastrous for our new driver, as it could be for WantItNow's company, if its employees are projecting messaging to the world without knowing what or how they should be projecting it. Additionally, one of the most important features in LinkedIn isn't even available when you first "start it up."

My WantItNow comparison helps to place in context that most valuable element of LinkedIn: its search capability. Just as our new driver's car will not run without filling the tank with gas, LinkedIn's Advanced People Search will not provide you with the results you seek if you have not first "filled" your account with the proper fuel, with that fuel being your actual network. Accurate and useful results require careful calibration of this sensitive search tool. And much like the relationship between your eyes and the lens of a telescope, only when your LinkedIn account is calibrated *to your actual network*, will you have your "aha" moment, unveiling LinkedIn's value to you.

Figure 4.1   LinkedIn's Advanced People Search Feature

LinkedIn has a structured search functionality that can target people, status updates, companies, jobs, answers, service providers, or groups. However, if you want to truly peer into your untapped network and find (or have served up to you) a particular "target" person, then the Advanced People Search is the way to go.

This feature is what has opened doors for me, including the front door to LinkedIn's headquarters (once I showed some of its investors the strategies we implement surrounding its search capabilities). And it's the one tool that made Todd Cieplinski, founder of digital solutions agency Universal Mind, say this:

"Dave showed me how to target and reach out to over 700 new leads, literally within minutes, using LinkedIn. The result was three customer deals closed within 90 days, totaling over $250K in new business."

To use the Advanced People Search feature in LinkedIn.com, click on the Advanced option on the top right side of the menu on any screen, as shown in Figure 4.1.

This brings you to a search screen that provides various options to select and adjust. The options available for input and selection in the free version of LinkedIn include Keywords, First/Last Name, Location, Title, Company, School, Industry, Relationship, and Language.[1] The tool then allows you to sort by Relevance, Relationship, Relationship and Recommendations, Connections, and Keywords.

This feature is best illustrated with an example. Let's say your target market includes CEOs in the computer software-related industries within 25 miles of Cambridge, Massachusetts, as shown in Figure 4.2:

- In the Title field, enter: "CEO" OR "Chief Executive Officer."
- In the Current or past menu below Title, click Current.
- Click on the Location bar and choose Located in or near.
- In the Postal Code section, enter "02138."
- Click on the area marked Within and choose 25 miles.

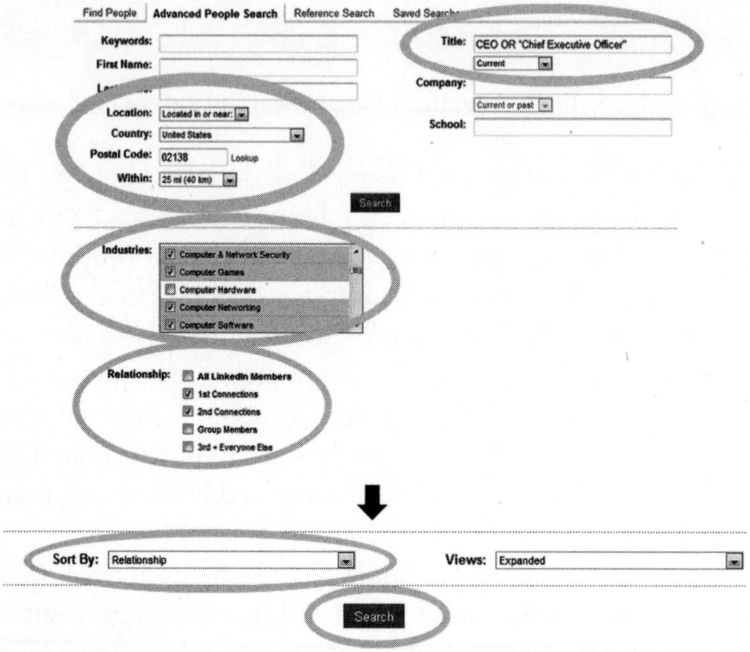

Figure 4.2   Example Advanced Search for CEOs

- Scroll through the Industries section and place a check mark next to Computer and Network Security, Computer Games, Computer Networking, and Software.
- Move to the Relationship section and select the areas marked 1st Degree Connections and 2nd Degree Connections.
- Click Sort By and choose Relationship.
- Click Search.

After you select Search, you will have in front of you a list of all the current CEOs in industries related to computer software within 50 miles of Cambridge, Massachusetts, sorted by relationship.

From top to bottom, you'll see a list of people who are either connected to you or connected to your connections (or you may see nobody, if you have not yet connected with enough relevant people). Under each 2nd degree connection appearing in this list, you will see an In Common section, indicating the number of connections whom you share with that potential "target" (if you don't

Figure 4.3 Advanced Search Mutual Connections

see this, just click on the person's name and you'll see your mutual connection(s) on the middle right side of their Profile). By clicking that link, you will see through whom you are connected to that person, as shown by the example in Figure 4.3. You may discover that you are connected through John OldRoommate or Jane Colleague to the CEO of a company you are trying to access. Either way, you now know who you need to contact to reach this key decision maker.

Let's stop there for a moment. Did you notice that this last paragraph just explained a key piece of game-changing technology that you can use *right now* (depending on the current state of your LinkedIn Profile—you may need to calibrate a few more key elements first)? What I'm teaching here is something I was invited to teach at Harvard Business School, MIT's Sloan School of Management, Babson's F.W. Olin Graduate School of Business, Dartmouth's Tuck School of Business, and many other well-respected educational institutions, clients, partners, nonprofits, and other organizations in various industries. The value here is pervasive throughout academia and the business world alike.

The takeaway is this: your search results will vary depending on the number and strength of your connections (and *their* connections). This particular search yielded almost 400 results in my network. As you grow and develop your LinkedIn network, you will find that your searches will generate increasingly more useful results. If I just opened a LinkedIn account, only had five 1st degree connections and performed this same search, I wouldn't get nearly as many results, even though my real-world network has over 1,000 1st degree connections. Despite having a highly polished professional Profile within this powerful network, you won't have access to this valuable information until you actually send or accept the *right* invitations in LinkedIn.

Remember to keep your search lens in mind: if you've never been a CEO or are not well-connected to many CEOs but are doing searches for them, you most likely won't get valuable results. Your company's CEO has a much better chance of receiving valuable information from these searches. Similarly, if you fulfill the recruiter function in your firm and perform a search for a specifically talented technologist to hire for your company, you will get results. However, the software engineer who works down the hall will likely yield more useful search results than your network, all other things being equal.

Once you have conducted a successful search, the second-stage magic happens: if you like the results of a search you conduct, you can save them and have continuously updated results of that search sent to your e-mail on a regular basis. By clicking the Save link at the top right of your search results, you will be given an option to have this information updated and sent to you by e-mail weekly, monthly, or never, as shown in Figure 4.4.

By opting for this e-mail, you essentially say, "Hey LinkedIn, I'd like you to send me a list of all decision makers currently leading companies in my target market, within 25 miles of my office. And if

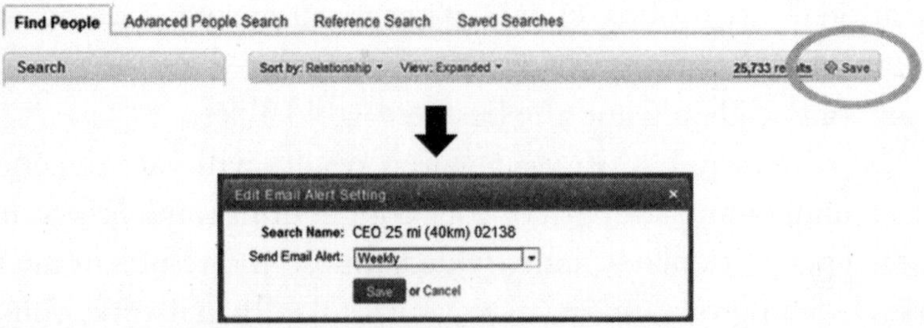

Figure 4.4   Save Advanced Search

you don't mind, sort them by the mutual connections whom I already know will make warm introductions for me to ensure that I am welcomed into those CEOs' offices." This concept of a "warm introduction" represents the exact opposite of a cold call, cold e-mail, or cold shoulder that you may get when approaching someone at a networking event whom you would like to know but have no immediate reason to want to know you. The current paradigm of networking expects the likelihood of this coldness. When used properly, LinkedIn permits you to proactively seek warm introductions in a manner that is not harassing to your personal network, therefore bringing warmth to much of what was cold in networking.

If, after performing the aforementioned search and after clicking Save, you don't think to return to LinkedIn.com in the following weeks, you will still continue to receive an updated list of relationship-sorted leads, because your current connections will add their own new connections. Imagine how many more warm introductions can be made available to you if you choose to stick with LinkedIn and grow your own LinkedIn network to reflect your real-world network. You'd be ushering in those new target market prospects who enter your online network on LinkedIn.

Those people who "enter your online network on LinkedIn" are not only those who just met someone you know in those past seven days (indicating a weak link). This newly added CEO on your list could have been a close friend of one of your neighbors for decades, but they *just* chose to connect on LinkedIn. So if your 1st degree connection, John OldFriend, connects with Steve Balmer next week, you can receive an e-mail alerting you that Microsoft's CEO is now one phone call away from you . . . *free*. If relationships help you to reach the people you target in your business, then this automated search will deliver to you arguably what is the best lead list ever on a weekly basis. You'll also save time by not having to dig up names and contact information for people you can cold call, because you can now give them a *warm call*.

Do take into consideration that your request for a warm introduction may not work out the first time you try. Don't be discouraged: just consider why it didn't work out and try again.

Keep this in mind as you answer the following question: How do you *currently* generate leads? This is not just a question for salespeople. If you're looking for a job, you want warm leads to employer prospects from people who know the best employers. If you're in a hiring function, you seek warm leads to the top passive candidates whom you'd like to convince to work for you. If you're in venture capital or private equity, you may want warm leads to high-quality deal flow or to chief investment officers at prospective limited partners. "Leads" can be applied to just about any job title or industry.

Do you buy phone or e-mail lists, mine for client contact data online, or hang around conferences and networking events to get and give business cards? Do you currently generate these leads based on who you can earn an introduction to through relationships you've built over years or just *get to* in a way that you wouldn't want people *getting* to you?

One of the clear commonalities between business and my military experiences is that reaching success does not include relying on hope as a viable strategy (you can see that Roger Staubach agrees with me on this point in the Foreword). So if you rely on hope to achieve your ongoing business goals, such as lead generation and effective hiring, these automated searches can be the drill sergeant who gently reminds you, on a weekly basis, of a much more effective course of action.

Help Yourself

As someone new to the greater Boston area in 2006, I knew it would be important to start forming meaningful relationships if I wanted my business to succeed. I was doing exciting things with LinkedIn, and there were a few important people in the area to whom I wanted to reach out—one of whom was Lee Hower. Lee was a venture capitalist at Point Judith Capital and one of LinkedIn's early employees. After searching in LinkedIn, I learned that I was only one phone call away from earning a warm introduction to Lee. That was to my well-connected friend, Bob Alperin.

Bob replied to my request: "Of course; I can't believe I didn't think of that sooner!" Let this statement serve as a reminder that people who are as successful and well-respected as Bob Alperin (who will therefore likely be connected to other successful people whom you may want to know), probably haven't built a relevant introduction spreadsheet mapping out how they can help you and everyone else they know.

Thanks to Bob's kind introduction, Lee invited me to his office, where I explained to him methods we use to help our clients with LinkedIn in ways I've found to be game-changing. Lee, a savvy venture capitalist (VC) and early LinkedIn employee, was impressed by what I had to say. I didn't realize just *how much* I had impressed him until Scott Kirsner used LinkedIn to check my references (unbeknownst to me) before writing a three-quarter page article on the topic that was featured on the front page of the *Boston Globe* business section. As you can imagine, these public comments very much helped my company demonstrate credibility, which led to shorter sales cycles and more significant interest from the top talent we pursued:

Make Better Introductions

By Scott Kirsner

September 6, 2009

Lee Hower knows a thing or two about using LinkedIn.

As a venture capitalist at Providence-based Point Judith Capital, Hower often uses the business networking site to check references on entrepreneurs whose companies he is considering as potential investments. Oh, and Hower was also part of the founding team of LinkedIn, reporting directly to the chief executive.

(continued)

> (*continued*)
>   Still, when Hower met with David Gowel, he admits he learned a few new tips and tricks. Gowel, a former Army Ranger who is also a kind of Jedi knight of LinkedIn. . .
>
> _____
>
> (Full article at: www.boston.com/business/articles/2009/09/06/make_better_introductions/)

There are many reasons to invest time in mastering LinkedIn. Although countless professionals have LinkedIn Profiles, many have no idea what to do with them, beyond hoping that it somehow helps them achieve their business goals. Even other books on the topic speak more about features than benefits and strategies; most don't yet realize the strategic implications of personal and organizational network mapping that is occurring through proper LinkedIn use. Some of LinkedIn's major benefits are camouflaged, and many struggle with the tool because of its nonintuitive applications in the traditional business context. I wasn't *always* a LinkedIn zealot, after all. There was a unique and interesting series of events that ultimately led me to this understanding, which changed my life . . . and gave me quite a story to tell.

Chapter 4 Summary

- One of LinkedIn's most valuable elements is its search capability, but it's an asset only when used by someone with a well-built Profile and an accurately mapped network.
- The Advanced Search feature can provide you relationship-sorted leads that are saved, regularly updated, and automatically sent to you, allowing you to dramatically shorten your current sales, hiring, fund-raising, or other business process cycles.
- When you grow your LinkedIn network to reflect your real-world network, it can lead to more high-quality introductions in a manner that is much more efficient than placing cold calls, attending networking events, or simply hoping for a lead to find you.

PART

2

From Army Ranger to LinkedIn Jedi

5

A Lesson in the Power of the Network

MY WIFE TOLD me that if I went back to Iraq, she'd shoot me. Although I hope she was kidding, at the end of 2006 my familial goals provided a compelling reason to consider a transition from active duty to civilian life: a task nearly as formidable for me as launching a new campaign in a hostile foreign land.

While serving in one of my Army positions in Germany in 2005, I met a general officer who changed the course of my life and to whom I'll be forever in social capital debt, Lieutenant General Gary Speer. I met General Speer because my direct boss at the time, Elizabeth Lim, had worked with him for a number of years at multiple military installations and wanted to personally introduce us so he could help shape my career. (This interaction is an example of how both who and what you know come into play; if she had a low opinion of me, Elizabeth would not have referred me to this highly respected leader in her network.)

At our first meeting, I informed General Speer that I was trying to find a way to extend my military career while also considering civilian options that could also fit in with my familial goals. One way to extend my time in uniform was to teach in an ROTC Program at a college campus in the United States. I explained that I had been exploring options for teaching in such a program in the Northeast, and he listened intently and reviewed my situation in depth, providing guidance and feedback on my approach.

I had already interviewed and been accepted by the professor and department head of my target school, and my current military unit was supportive of this transition. I just hadn't found the success necessary to navigate through the Army's bureaucratic personnel channels that could release me from my current unit and allow me to join my new one. This proposed career path was an atypical one for a junior military officer—one requiring an exception to policy. That exception was something I failed to achieve even after the exhaustive efforts I took over a six-month period to use the system and win over someone with enough rank to grant it.

After sharing this with General Speer, and after he thoroughly reviewed my situation, I watched in awe as the power of my network exploded in front of me.

With a sincere note to a friend he had known for over thirty years who was in the position to approve this exception request, General Speer asked that if ethically and reasonably appropriate, I be considered for that ROTC position I desired. I saw mountains moved in the ridgeline of bureaucracy, and within days, I received orders to become an assistant professor of Military Leadership at MIT.

Being assigned that position was the result of being a hardworking, value-producing, ethical soldier surrounded by people with strong networks. But in many ways, I got lucky. I didn't know that General Speer could introduce me to the person who could approve my request for the exception to policy. Had I (and he) already been on LinkedIn, this victory from my network would have been much easier to obtain. I could have performed a quick search on my targeted decision maker and asked for the introduction. But the process of getting that position got my gears turning about the need for a better way to use the network in which I existed. I had always assumed that if I worked hard and long enough, nothing could stand in the way of accomplishing my goals. However, I had spent the better part of a year trying as hard as I could, in vain, to accomplish something that I could have achieved in a couple of weeks, if I knew then what I know now about LinkedIn.

As if this new position wasn't good enough, the job came with a significant perk: location, location, location. MIT is situated in the heart of Kendall Square (one of the most rapidly developing innovation clusters on the planet), just a duck tour boat ride across the Charles River from Boston. While working with some of the top minds in the country at MIT—and among corporate neighbors like Google, Microsoft, and Akamai—it was hard to ignore the communication revolution occurring around me. The fact that many of the students I taught were from Facebook's birthplace was the icing on the cake, and it is what ultimately transformed me from being a social media critic (good story to follow) into a LinkedIn zealot. I watched from an uncommon vantage point as Facebook evolved into a household name. I also recognized that it was rapidly changing communications behavior for the future of business, as all my students at these different schools (through ROTC, I actually taught at seven campuses around Boston) were addicted to it. And it showed no signs of letting up.

Amos, I Stand Corrected

A key to building social capital is the importance of having both the ability to admit when you're wrong and an eagerness to accept and react to criticism. And this excerpt allows me to demonstrate and do just that.

While still on active duty, and before I was permitted to teach anything to anyone at MIT, I was required to attend the Advanced Officer Course in Fort Knox, Kentucky. While there, I was fortunate to train and learn with a talented group of leaders, one by the name of Captain Amos Oh.

Amos was one of the clear leaders in our class of captains. Because Amos was an Innovator (as you'll see in Chapter 12),

(continued)

(*continued*)

who was heavily using this new online platform called Facebook, I made it an ongoing mission to make fun of Amos at every chance. I would taunt him on a regular basis about his *foolish* use of social media, making references to his lack of marital status, suggesting parallels between Amos and the undesirables that are showcased on NBC's series "To Catch a Predator." He would laugh coolly and shake off my ribbings, saying, "Dave, just wait until you get to MIT; I guarantee that you will recognize the value of social media."

I could absolutely fight the futile battle by saying "Uh, well, I don't consider LinkedIn to be social media, and therefore I was right." However, since those exact Facebook interactions that he referenced opened my eyes to what LinkedIn *was not*, I stand (at the position of attention) corrected. Therefore, as I grow a business founded to help people adopt social technologies faster, I would like to let Amos (and the world) know that he was right, and I was wrong.

How I Got LinkedIn

During my time in higher education, I realized that despite having a cushy, nondeployable position teaching at one of the world's top academic institutions, I was still putting an outrageous amount of time into a job that, although personally satisfying, was not bringing me closer to achieving my family's goals. So, although it was an incredible position, I started looking for a new career and found LinkedIn the same way that most people do—by job hunting.

For Those Seeking Jobs

The majority of the value that is discovered through effective LinkedIn use lies *outside* of the job search arena. Despite this, many people first engage in LinkedIn through job searching, so it's not a digression to explain some of the key concepts learned while doing just that—concepts that are relevant even for those who are not currently on the hunt.

I discovered LinkedIn's power while looking for two things: a civilian job and people who could give me valuable advice about whether or not to start my own business. And because I approached my search from both of those perspectives, it gave me so much more than I expected. Here are some considerations about using LinkedIn when you're seeking employment, as well as some generally useful networking tips:

1. **Reach out by giving, not requesting:** Being out of work is one of your greatest opportunities to build (and not cash in on) social capital, because, by definition, you have extra time on your hands. One way to spend it wisely is to make thoughtful introductions for others. Think about the people in your network who might be able to help you in your search, and then decide who you could connect them to in your network by using the LinkedIn tools we discuss in this book. Offer to make that introduction, always keeping in mind the need to treat your friend or colleague as an end, and not a *means* to an end. If you stimulate a high-quality connection for people, they may turn around and make a good introduction for you. Or even better, they may have a position for you outright once they see what you are able to bring to the table without having to be asked.

2. **Arrive with value:** What is one of the most compelling things that an interviewee could do during an interview? Imagine if you were interviewing someone who sat down and said, "I looked at your company's website, studied your value proposition, and thought of someone in your target market I know named Jane WarmLead, whom I think you should meet. Here's her business card; she's expecting your call." This interviewee performed her due diligence, digested your value proposition, and did for you what every company ultimately wants its employees to do or to facilitate: she generated new business. It would be hard to *not* ask this person back for another interview.

3. **Understand that decision makers make decisions:** In addition to focusing on the elements of LinkedIn's Jobs section, perform an Advanced People Search for CEOs, presidents, or other decision makers in your industry, regardless of what's on their job boards. When you get a meeting with John TopDog, start off by saying, "TopDog, since you're an executive in the industry I want to work in, I'd love to know what you think about my approach to getting hired." TopDog might then think of someone you'd work perfectly with and make an introduction to one of his peers; or he may even decide to hire you himself. Given the current state of the world economy, it may also be beneficial to tell a company that you're willing to begin work on a part-time or an intern basis so that you have a chance to demonstrate how much value you can provide before coming on full-time. This could be your foot in the door that turns into a full-time position.

4. **Be a team player first:** What do you do if you're at a job and don't want your boss to know you're looking for another job? How do you handle that in LinkedIn? First, remember that LinkedIn is a public tool with many millions of people using it. Writing "seeking new position" in your headline wouldn't be the most discreet way to job search. Instead, ensure that you shape your Profile so that you're seen as a candidate that *any* employer would desire. A useful way to show that you're a team player is by populating the Recommendations section of your Profile. If your colleagues and superiors say glowing things about you, why wouldn't other employers want you on *their* teams? It's your job to tailor your messaging to include keywords that your specific audience is searching for, as well as those that they'll find compelling when they read your Profile. Then you can suggest that potential employers visit your LinkedIn Profile when you send your resume out in confidence. This will allow them to see that you're not going to give up and cash out on your job just because you're searching for another one, which is something that prospective employers generally appreciate.

Long before I knew about LinkedIn, needed a job, or even graduated from West Point, I recognized that social capital could be traded in very tangible ways when done properly. To demonstrate this, I have a story to tell about a time when I was looking for the fast lane but instead found myself going nowhere fast.

Automatic Social Capital

As a military academy cadet, you could track the level of social capital I held in my coffers on a weekly basis by the caliber of car I was driving when I left Thayer Gate, the military academy campus's "front door," each weekend. This odd indicator is due to the restriction that cadets are not permitted to own a vehicle at West Point until after spring break of Cow Year (now would be a good time to explain that West Point freshmen are labeled *plebes*, sophomores go by *yearling* or *yuk*, juniors are *cows*, and the seniors prepare for graduation and commissioning as *firsties*). So, to enjoy college life beyond West Point's walls, I had to improvise. Working toward my BS in economics as a lowly plebe, I quickly identified some supply and demand issues surrounding me:

> Dave had zero cars *versus* Dave wanted more than zero cars.
>
> Firsties had cars *and* Firsties wanted someone to clean their cars.

Economics and a newfound talent for cleaning everything I owned in preparation for weekly white-glove room inspections initiated my days of car borrowing. The first car I borrowed with some friends was a 20-year-old Volvo with a few flaws. When we arrived in the parking lot to see this (not so) hot rod, the car had a flat tire and dead battery. Even after fixing those issues, the trip managed to get worse when the engine caught fire at a gas station. But this minor flare-up was

(continued)

(*continued*)

nothing compared to the moment when the front left tire detached from the car and rolled into the woods while the Volvo was moving at about 65 miles per hour.

The next car I borrowed was a Jeep Wrangler that appeared to have been built during WWI or perhaps the Civil War era (evidently, the story of losing a wheel on the highway didn't make the guy with the Porsche want to offer me his keys). This car played a fun game where the dashboard lights would go out—all of them—whenever they felt like it. So while driving at night, and in the rain, I had to stop at a rest area to buy a flashlight so my copilot could let me know how fast I was travelling and if the engine was overheating. Determined to avoid condemnation to a cadet-hood of borrowing cars that would nearly kill me (or repel any potential candidates for the title of Mrs. Gowel), I set out to build some social capital. Before returning the *Jeep of Darkness* to its lender, I vacuumed it, washed it, filled it with gas (even though I borrowed it running on fumes), and delivered the keys back to the owner in a timely manner. This earned me a, "Wow. Thanks, Gowel."

The following week, I proactively approached John Jeep-Guy and inquired, "Sir, can I borrow your car this weekend?" When he replied that he'd happily do so again if he wasn't using it himself, I persisted, "Do you know of anyone staying on post who has a car and might want it cleaned, washed, and gassed up?" To that he replied, "Yeah, I think John IntrepidCow has a paper to write. I'll shoot him a note." After seeing JeepGuy hit Send on his computer, I walked down the hall and knocked three times (at the Academy, when visiting a superior's office or room, you must knock three times on the door; when visiting a subordinate, you knock twice). At IntrepidCow's barracks door I asked if I could borrow his car. Looking up from JeepGuy's e-mail, he replied that his car actually could use some detailing, but he couldn't loan it to me because he had to get the brakes fixed. Seeing an opening, I offered to drop it off for him at the dealer when I arrived at my destination. This earned me the keys to his newer model Dodge Intrepid and another chance to lay a foundation of social capital with a car-owning cadet at the Academy.

After that second positive exchange, word of mouth spread, and people actually started to let me borrow *new* cars—all because of the positive reputation that arose from the way I took care of loaned vehicles.

Then one day, long after my car-borrowing social capital had been built up around the Academy, I heard two knocks on my door. After jumping to the position of attention and calling out, "Enter sir or ma'am," my door slowly opened and I saw JeepGuy standing there. "Hey Gowel, do you want to borrow my Jeep this weekend? It could really use a good vacuuming," he optimistically offered. To this I replied, "No thank you, Sir, I've already found someone to lend me a car this weekend." I said this as I glanced down at my desk at the keys to a brand-new BMW M3 convertible—borrowed, of course.

Much like the rest of the world, you may not see the magic in LinkedIn right away. If you are only beginning to use it now, know that it takes time. After devoting a substantial number of months to using it and making many mistakes, from which we now shield our clients, I began to appreciate this platform's revolutionary aspects. I also discovered that the world just didn't understand it the same way that I did. This realization led me to devote much time to developing my network and subsequently formalizing a methodology for appropriate, professional LinkedIn etiquette (a methodology that actually resonates with professionals instead of causing them concern). It was then that I began to grasp the fact that this tool not only could be something that would help me find a job but that could actually *create* my job.

From Clearly Creative's earliest days, we recognized that our LinkedIn training prowess was a unique way to attract clients who would then recognize our value and hire us for overall marketing strategy consulting. LinkedIn then became a line of business, which led to the successes that in turn became the foundation for RockTech. It's important to note that none of this would have happened without a lot of help from many wonderful advisors, friends, investors, and business partners, who helped me chart (and often correct) my course.

Chapter 5 Summary

- Through the social capital that I built with my army leaders, I received material, bureaucratic-lifting introductions that assigned me to what became a life-changing position at MIT.
- I started using LinkedIn to find a job. I soon realized that it was much more than a job search tool, and I used that knowledge to start my civilian career.
- If you are using LinkedIn for a job search, consider:
    1. Using LinkedIn with the intention of making introductions before requesting them.
    2. Arriving with something of relational value when networking or interviewing.
    3. Targeting corporate decision makers closely connected to you for: feedback on your approach, warm introductions, or perhaps even a job that can be built for you.
    4. Demonstrating through your Profile and actions that you are a team player.

6

Well-Connected Connections

Just Do It

When I chose to leave the military, I had to make a decision: get a job or start a business. Did I want to follow my passion right out of the gate, putting my family at the financial risk of living through the ups and downs of an entrepreneur's paycheck (if such a thing even exists)? Or did I want to use my military-grown leadership skills by running a business after climbing the corporate ladder? I knew that building my network would be the key to finding the answer. What I didn't know was that I would meet some of the most influential people in my career—and in my lifetime—by using LinkedIn. Many such advisors shaped who I became as a professional, and some of them even pushed me to decide to start a business in tough economic times. One of my extraordinary mentors is Marshall N. Carter.

I first met Marsh when he served as a guest speaker for a military leadership course I was teaching at MIT's Sloan School of Management. The class's primary focus was to teach civilian students about elements of combat leadership so they could glean some of our experiences without having to endure a combat zone themselves. To this end, we invited impressive guest lecturers who experienced leadership in both military and civilian environments. Marsh—current Chairman of the New York Stock Exchange, former Navy Cross and Purple Heart recipient who served in the Vietnam War, and West Point graduate—was one such guest speaker. Having been turned down by 85 employers upon completion of his military service in the United States Marine Corps (you may recall that Americans were not as supportive of our forces during the Vietnam conflict as they have been in recent times), Marsh lent his experiences to veterans like myself, who were considering a civilian career following their military service.

Over the course of that year, Marsh became a trusted advisor of mine. He is ultimately the person who told me to seize the chance to run with my business idea, a recommendation that was atypical of others at that time. Many other advisors would regularly ask a series of questions about my interests and skills, often prompting me to figure out for myself what decisions I would make. Though this was tremendously helpful, it resonated like a lone rifle firing before dawn when Marsh broke from my advisory pack and told me he thought it was the right time and I was in the right business. That year, in 2007, my wife, Julie, and I chose to start our marketing firm, Clearly Creative, in order to help companies integrate new forms of communication with the traditional methods: foreshadowing the path that led us here today.

Capital from Kurzina

Marsh also grew social capital stores with me by introducing me to Peter Kurzina. Marsh was guest teaching in a class one day for Peter and suggested that I attend, as he thought it would be useful in my endeavors. By being placed in front of Peter with the Marsh Carter stamp of approval, this new contact welcomed me warmly.

Peter had worked in crisis management for 33 years before becoming a popular senior lecturer at MIT's Sloan School of Management, where he teaches, among other courses, Managing in Adversity and Corporations at the Crossroads: The CEO

Perspective. I thought it would simply be an insightful class taught by someone with some amazing experiences. I didn't realize that over the next few years, Peter would both advise me and lead me to a countless number of essential relationships. I would certainly not be where I am now without his generous (and repeated) insights and introductions that all started with a *social capital loan* from Marsh Carter. I did my best to impress Peter right off the bat; after all, a first impression is where you start to lay the foundation for your social capital trade with any new acquaintance. It's important to pay attention and be willing to help those who help you, especially if you want to prove you're worth an investment of their time. When first meeting Peter, I did just that. To make conversation after hearing of my military background, Peter explained that he had been in the military when he first started his career. He casually noted that he had loved the belts that came with the uniforms. He also mentioned that he couldn't purchase another one, as civilians are not permitted to buy them. Since I had a few extra belts and felt that it would not be a breach of national security to give him a couple, the next time we met, I handed him two. Peter's gratitude was quickly visible through his reaction. The fact that I had actually listened to what Peter said and was thoughtful enough to do something like that for someone I had just met, built social capital with him. Now, keep in mind, it *felt good* to give Peter something that brought him happiness. I really enjoyed meeting him that first time and had no idea of the role he could play in my business' success. A key structural consideration in building social capital is focusing on the former and less on the latter: seek the *social* element of building relationships and let the more tangible *capital* element evolve where appropriate.

When looking to have my LinkedIn knowledge tested by my most senior and successful mentors, Peter agreed to have coffee with me at our office and to critique me while I provided him a LinkedIn training session. He understood immediately that I was teaching something revolutionary, and he quickly became one of my strongest allies. Since that time, he has ushered me into the warm contact of many highly influential people within MIT and beyond, in some very well-known organizations. He simply explains in his introductions that he thinks we would mutually enjoy meeting one another. In Peter's (and all my advisors') eyes, it has to be a win-win proposition for all parties involved to put his personal brand on the line.

Word of mouth is helpful, but it is far more valuable when coming from the *right* mouth. If my mom was going to the same people and saying the same things about me that Peter did, I probably wouldn't have been as well received, as mom is slightly biased. Peter's gratis introductions were far preferable than any purchased cold call list, e-mail list, or trade show I could have attended.

The business conundrum here is that while word of mouth is truly the best form of marketing, you can't buy it; it can only be earned. If I were to offer Peter any sum of money to make those same introductions, he'd instantly deny me, because of the ethical violation of selling something as valuable and important as his personal seal of approval. His network expects that he would only make introductions to people from whom they will also benefit in some way.

As you'll see in the next few paragraphs, each of the following people to whom Peter introduced me made separate, unique comments that resonated with me, shaping the way we now train people on using LinkedIn. One of those people was Ken Morse. As former head of the MIT Entrepreneurship Center (E-Center), Ken is very busy and a pretty good guy to know. He regularly travels around the world, teaching entrepreneurship to those fortunate enough to be in his audience. When I was introduced to Ken, he came to my office to learn why Peter was so insistent that Ken and I meet. The first hours of our relationship were spent discussing my and LinkedIn's respective business strategies. We dove deeply into both the platform and my business consultation model. Some time later, after we transitioned from a consultative business model into the software model that reaches many more people than we could ever before, Ken made an interesting observation that summarized his thoughts on our business: "Dave, what you are building here is not just a new business but a new category of business."

Peter also introduced me to the aforementioned Bill Aulet, Ken's successor as the managing director of MIT's E-Center. This meeting was notable because, given his position at the E-Center, Bill sees a lot of business ideas in various stages. He is bombarded with concepts—from the great to the not-so-great and everything in between—on a daily basis. Bill listened to how I believed LinkedIn would change business forever and the role my company would play in doing so. Social media was popular at the time, so I suspect that of all the business ideas Bill had heard, many were focused on these new platforms and applications. But after I finished explaining one element of my training that he found personally valuable, he stopped and said something that resonated with me in a profound way: "*Whoa, this isn't social.*" At that moment, he understood the professional impact LinkedIn could deliver.

Another fantastic introduction from Peter was to MIT Professor Howard Anderson. Howard founded the Yankee Group (a consulting firm that focuses on the global connectivity of enterprises), cofounded Battery Ventures (a technology-driven venture capital firm), ascended to a professorship at MIT Sloan, and has been involved in the successes of many companies throughout his life. In his introduction, Peter explained that Howard's LinkedIn Profile was not up to Peter's newfound standards and asked that I assist Howard in fixing his personal LinkedIn site.

I sat down with Howard and in about 45 minutes convinced him that LinkedIn was going to change sales, one of Howard's areas of expertise. After our meeting, he submitted the following Recommendation, which is now visible on my Profile: "In less than an hour, Dave showed me why LinkedIn is the best online tool for lead generation and personal marketing. I even asked him to guest teach a class on the subject to my MBA students at Sloan. He knows his stuff."

The social capital you earn can quickly turn into hard capital when a potential client sees that you've earned praise from a highly respected leader in your industry. Having endorsements on your LinkedIn Profile helps you shorten sales cycles and generate new and warm leads. Even if John Research is performing his due diligence on you and hasn't had the pleasure of knowing your endorsers personally, he can quickly learn of their successes via their Profiles—especially if they have such reputations as the folks Peter has introduced me to—and potentially more informatively, see any mutual contacts he may have with them.

After getting positive feedback from so many whom I had just met by utilizing my LinkedIn skills, it was time to get some answers. Why were there so few out there who really understood LinkedIn? Why hadn't the world woken up and taken notice more actively? Maybe LinkedIn didn't have a mechanism to bring a scalable and effective training model to market or felt it wasn't the time to do so. If so, could my team produce a platform that could deliver such training in a manner to scale to the size capable of impacting millions or hundreds of millions of people? These questions intrigued me, so I used LinkedIn to get answers from LinkedIn's executives themselves.

Chapter 6 Summary

- Seeking advisors can often be more valuable than seeking a job or a new client. You can use LinkedIn to surround yourself with people who can not only provide you with advice, but who can also critique you on the quality of advice that you give others (if that is something you do). Do keep in mind that giving advice is an art, and for many people, a great way to *lose* social capital is to give too much advice.
- Strive for the balance of being able to actively look for relevant introductions while remaining comfortable with telling someone that an introduction is an imperfect fit. Peter Kurzina, one of my advisors and introducers, does this well.
- It is easiest to win people over upon your first meeting with them if you take the time to do your homework on them first. When I initially met with Howard Anderson, I knew LinkedIn's capability to revolutionize sales would be interesting to him because of the classes he taught and from talking to his students.

7

When Recommendations Are Powerful

IT DIDN'T TAKE long to realize that in order to really get somewhere with LinkedIn, it would be helpful to reach the company itself. So, of course, I sought out Reid Hoffman, LinkedIn's founder. Using a LinkedIn search in 2009, I found that Reid was a 3rd degree connection of mine: Someone I knew was connected to someone else who knew Reid. That connection was Steve Snyder, Entrepreneur-in-Residence at Gesmer Updegrove LLP. When I asked him to search for Reid, by using LinkedIn Steve identified his mutual connection to Reid as Jeff Bussgang, author of *Mastering the VC Game*, cofounder of college savings site Upromise, and general partner at Flybridge Capital Partners.

Steve had very positive things to say about Jeff and thought we'd get along well. Soon after Steve made the introduction, Jeff invited me to his office to meet. Not only did Jeff know Reid (who provided an interview for Jeff's book), but Jeff also knew LinkedIn, as he had joined the site within the first six months of its existence.

Aside from identifying him as a potential avenue to connect with Reid, I also concluded that Jeff's VC firm fit into our target market as a potential client. However, I watched that potential start to slip away when, during our first meeting, Jeff asked me what I thought of LinkedIn's iPhone app. Being a BlackBerry user, I admitted not knowing much about it (BlackBerries weren't supported by a LinkedIn app at the time).

Here I was, conversing with a well-respected entrepreneur who cofounded and sold the largest private source of college funding contributions in the United States and wrote a book about mastering his industry, and in that moment I didn't even have a word to say about a popular application for this platform in which I was supposedly an expert. I sensed Jeff's interest in me as an entrepreneur shift toward politeness, likely out of respect for Steve, the social capital trader who risked his brand to get me that meeting with Jeff.

Like any good Ranger, I recognized the moment I began to lose ground and thrust onward to gain it back, so I queried, "How well do you feel your firm is using LinkedIn collectively?" Jeff paused to consider the question. Sensing an opening, I sent more troops toward the summit: "If you're not sure everyone on your team leverages this tool as well as you do, would you consider having me help them get there through some training?"

"How about this," he started. "If you can teach me something valuable in LinkedIn, I'll hire you to take all my partners through your training." I didn't hesitate to reply, "Great; should we do it here or in your office?" Jeff curiously said, "Really, you want to do it *right now?*"

Within that final 15 minutes of our initial meeting, I went to Jeff's office and dove deeply into the more Advanced features and strategies of LinkedIn while directly tying them to benefits of deal flow, due diligence, talent attraction, and utility for Jeff's portfolio companies. Looking up from his computer, he said with a grin, "Dave, this has been great. I look forward to working with you."

This was a significant moment of clarity. I had proved to myself that LinkedIn was not only going to change business, but it was going to change my life. Jeff was an avid early adopter of LinkedIn, who is a master of his technological space. Therefore, if I could show *him* the value of our offering, I had to suppose that the number of people who were still in the dark on the topic must be staggering.

That first meeting with Jeff, which had come about from my effective use of LinkedIn's search capabilities, set into motion a series of introductions that contributed to the success our company enjoys today. Ironically, one of those introductions was *not* to Reid Hoffman, the man I initially set out to meet through my meeting with Jeff. Jeff was giving me so much value as a client and through his word-of-mouth support that I didn't want to seem ungrateful by harassing him for an introduction he might not have seen as a good fit at the time. Although I didn't immediately get the introduction to Reid Hoffman that I had initially sought through Jeff, I still wanted to get to LinkedIn.

I soon realized that an intro to someone as busy, popular, and accomplished as Reid probably wasn't something I should request from people I'd just met; I would have to work hard and build much social capital to earn it. Plus, I wouldn't want to be introduced to him until I had something worthy of his time to discuss. I ultimately met Reid through Eve Phillips—a friend and entrepreneur who made the decision that I would represent her brand well in front of an industry icon like Reid. Judging by the fact that I not only had the opportunity to meet with Reid but also built such a great partnership with LinkedIn, I would say that she was right.

Some Interesting AdVentures

At Jeff's recommendation, I met with Flybridge Capital's vice president of Marketing, Kate Castle, shortly after my meeting with Jeff to see how we could bring our LinkedIn offerings to her organization. Her resultant support and enthusiasm for Clearly Creative's services opened many doors for us and resulted in closed business deals and other opportunities. Kate then made two very significant introductions for me, the first to Emily Mendell, vice president of strategic affairs at the National Venture Capital Association (NVCA). A communications leader in the venture capital (VC) world, Emily hired us to work with the NVCA. Later that year, she invited us to speak at one of their national conferences in Silicon Valley.

As the VC world started to wake up to the alarm we were ringing thanks to the double espresso shot of LinkedIn served up to them by Clearly Creative—Kate also introduced me to Stephanie Carter, marketing and communications partner at ABS Capital Partners. Stephanie initially hired us to train one of the junior members of her marketing team on using LinkedIn. It was fairly common when we first started delivering our services for leadership to have this in mind: "Oh, you teach social media? Sure, we'll have one of our more *social media-savvy* (younger) team members take the training and explain it to our *less savvy* (older) leaders." The challenge to this philosophy is that since LinkedIn is a thousand-blade Swiss Army knife, it's not realistic to expect a junior member of the team to be able to grasp the strategic implications of the tool and then re-package and deliver them to others, especially when tasked as an additional duty.

It was after seeing me present to the larger NVCA group in Silicon Valley (thanks to Emily) that Stephanie decided to hire us to train her partners at ABS Capital Partners on more effective LinkedIn usage. Because of that meeting's success, they also brought me to Chicago to speak about LinkedIn for all ABS's port-folio companies later in the year.

Then, in mid-2010, Stephanie, Emily, and I were brought in as speakers at a Private Equity International (PEI) Conference in New York City. I was invited to speak based on the growing suc-cess we were having in delivering LinkedIn throughout the VC and private equity communities.

Since I've known them, Stephanie and Emily have both made valuable introductions for my company. One such intro-duction came during the conference's initial panel, in which they were both participants. Stephanie was asked to speak about what she did for ABS Capital in terms of the firm's brand expansion and marketing over the past year. For the first three-quarters of her address, she didn't mention anything about our company, and I was starting to wonder if I mistook their enthu-siastic reaction to my session as something it wasn't.

Near the end of Stephanie's review of ABS's year, she looked up at me in the back of the auditorium and said, "Dave, I'm about to give you a very good commercial." Returning her attention to the group, she announced, "You're going to hear from Dave Gowel later today. We hired him to take ABS through LinkedIn at one of our quarterly meetings, and I have never seen my partners so excited and motivated about *any* similar training before. They have been using LinkedIn dramatically more effectively than before and have found tremendous benefit from Dave's training."

Shortly after hearing Stephanie's comments, Emily broke from her scheduled remarks as the emcee and let the audience know that she too had been impressed with what we were doing for her organization on the LinkedIn front.

These sincerely earned testimonials resulted in far more business than what we would have received had we gone the traditional route of paying for an exhibit booth at that conference. Instead of hoping to sell our services to the audience during the breaks between sessions, we were a main event, introduced by clients who gave a referral to 120 members of our target market in two synchronized cannon-like shots. Having respected leaders like Stephanie and Emily present us to that group in such a positive light reinforced our thought leadership and provided remarkable business value.

Getting Recommendations

Stephanie's and Emily's testimonials were compelling and impactful to the attendees in my target market in the room that day. Imagine if you could get compelling endorsements for yourself in a place where everyone in your network can see them, such as a LinkedIn Recommendation. For me in LinkedIn, that network currently consists of over 10 million people, including my 1st, 2nd, and 3rd degree connections. We've already discussed how Google values LinkedIn Profiles, which means that most people searching for information on you will be a couple of clicks away from compelling testimonials about you, *if* you care to ask for them (and do so in the right way). This is the one and only section of your LinkedIn Profile where *other* people talk about you, which most people would agree is better than you talking about yourself.

Some people believe having Recommendations on their Profiles suggests an air of desperation and indicates that they are not happy where they are in life and are seeking new opportunities. Others have dozens of Recommendations, ranging from novel-like soliloquies on their extensive professional background to poorly proofed comments about their golf skills from an old college friend. It's easy to list your accomplishments and the value you provide to your target audience, but when your connections tell people you're an expert in a concise, compelling way, it resonates much more clearly.

The inclinations of your target market should influence how you ask for and display Recommendations on your Profile. Once you've identified what is compelling to them, find someone you know well who resembles your target market (such as a satisfied client or business partner) and ask them for a Recommendation.

Similar to requesting an introduction, you should generally make this request for a social favor in a manner that you feel will be comfortably received. This may be accomplished through e-mail, a phone call, or another form of communication if you don't feel your target market is comfortable using LinkedIn's standard Get Recommended feature. In order to reduce some of the time it takes for your target to complete this favor, you may compose a concise recommendation that describes your relationship with that business partner. It may be less forward if you indicate that he should feel free to edit, delete, or change any portion of it. As an example, when asking for a Recommendation, you can say something like:

"Hey John, I enjoyed working with you on our last project, and since you have made the comments summarized in the paragraph below, would you mind submitting this (or editing as you see fit) as a LinkedIn Recommendation for me? I just got into LinkedIn and feel as if I'm missing something without a well-respected client like you confirming what I say about myself. I don't want to be too forward; I just thought I'd type this up to save you time since I'm asking for this favor. Of course, if you're not comfortable doing so for any reason, feel free to disregard without any need for an explanation . . . "

If you deem that writing a recommendation about yourself is too bold for you or your target market, you might include a variation of this by sending along some bullets of what you'd like your contact to say about you. The bottom line is that you want to have influence over the message that your contacts spread. You could just ask for a Recommendation from someone, but you risk getting back a paragraph that talks only about one aspect of what you have to offer. Although that may be appreciated, if it's not exactly the talent that you want your current target market to hear about you, it could mean a lost opportunity. You want to control your message as best you can in a world where everyone has a (searchable) voice about you and your business, and this is a good way to start.

The other way you can acquire LinkedIn Recommendations is by giving to others something similar to what you are hoping to receive. If you give Jane Praiseworthy a Recommendation and she chooses to share it on her Profile, the first thing LinkedIn does is propose that Jane return the favor to you. This can be perceived as a somewhat guilt-laden approach and therefore not the preferred method; however, if you've performed quality work for someone who just hasn't thought to thank you publicly yet, it can help you to gain by first giving.

People in your network who view your Profile can see who has recommended you. They can click on your recommender's Profile and therefore have the opportunity to check out his or her background, something we could never accomplish easily (and therefore may never have done) with traditional business references.

As for the type of the Recommendations you should display, here are a few things to think about:

- The number (and length) of Recommendations you would take the time to read about somebody else
- Having an extraordinary amount of Recommendations pushes down information throughout the rest of your Profile, and may prevent people from getting to other important experiences you want to display
- The priorities and interests of your target market

LinkedIn prompts you to obtain multiple Recommendations, as its Profile meter will only reach 100 percent completion once you have three. But this doesn't mean that your Profile is incomplete without them, and you shouldn't concern yourself with getting Recommendations just to satisfy what someone else deems to be a complete Profile. If you decide that Recommendations are for you, then display those that are highly relevant to your target market. For example, if you currently have a total of 25 Recommendations, you can choose to exhibit the handful that you believe would resonate most with the people in your network. If Reid Hoffman, Warren Buffett, or Bill Gates were to connect with you via LinkedIn and write a Recommendation for you, you may choose to remove otherwise valuable information from your Profile so your viewers would gravitate toward just one or two platinum testimonials. Keep in mind that you can show, hide, or request other Recommendations as your target market evolves.

Instead of making you appear needy for others' approval, Recommendations can allow you to showcase your talent, appear credible, and show the world that it's not only *you* who values your services. Remember, people in your network can see those Recommendations, so if you are concerned about the privacy of those with whom you connect (such as protecting your clients from a competitor's view), then it may not be in your best interest to gather and post Recommendations from certain people.

LinkedIn is not just a place for you to demonstrate professional competence. If you've already displayed the amazing things you've done on your Profile for your target market to view, Recommendations on LinkedIn can also go a long way toward communicating that you're actually a good or personable team player as well. There are many highly accomplished professionals who look like a perfect fit *on paper* but come across very differently in person. Therefore, realize that asking someone who is a friend and business partner to provide a Recommendation—one that mentions your likability or teamwork mind-set—may nicely augment your educational pedigree or professional accomplishments.

Recommendation FAQs

What considerations should flow through your mind when you've been asked to give a Recommendation for someone else? This isn't difficult if you know and like the person requesting said Recommendation. But of course, you are not always approached by your favorite employee or best friend. Here are a few questions I've answered on this topic along the way:

Q: I manage a large group of people and am often asked to give Recommendations to people I like; I just don't have the time to write them. What should I do?

A: Give the requester some homework (after all, they asked you for a favor) by using this template or one like it: "John Good-Student, it would be a pleasure to recommend you. Since I've been extraordinarily busy lately but want to get this to you in a timely fashion and provide a helpful Recommendation, please draft up an appropriate recommendation for me to edit and paste into LinkedIn. I'll review at it as soon as I can!"

Q: I'm considering looking for another job but don't want to advertise that fact to the world (or more specifically, my current employer). How do I use Recommendations to help me achieve this covert mission?

A: Employers usually seek team players, so giving Recommendations to your teammates at your current position (with the potential that they'll reciprocate by returning the favor) could work more effectively than walking around the office asking for Recommendations. If you want to approach your boss, you might do so by suggesting that you think it would be good for your clients (or other departments, constituents, higher leaders, and so forth) to see that there's a 360-degree environment of respect throughout your office and division. This would make it appropriate for everyone to propose relevant Recommendations to that boss for her review and submission (but if you see *The Power in a Link* on her desk, you may want to vary a bit from this approach, or rip this page out of her book).

Q: What if I don't think the person seeking a Recommendation deserves one? Or I don't want to weaken my brand by recommending a subpar performer, but I still have to work with him or have a personal relationship outside the office? If I am not comfortable being candid, telling the requester I don't feel comfortable recommending his work, how can I get out of this socially awkward situation?

A: There are a few options—some slightly more realistic than others, depending on your personality:

1. Give credit only where it's due. To protect your brand but keep from burning a personal relationship, provide a concise Recommendation highlighting whatever positive traits the person displays, bypassing any statements of substance that would appeal to the requester's target market. This could be as simple as "I've worked with Jane for three years at our office in Denver. I've always enjoyed chatting with her at the water cooler and I could always count on a funny e-mail forward from her."
2. Just ignore the request. Some people often ask for a large number of Recommendations on LinkedIn and may not even notice if you don't respond.
3. Ask the requester to draft up a Recommendation that "reflects some details of your working relationship" so you can provide him an effective Recommendation. He may start thinking about those details of his performance in your relationship, or lack thereof, and choose to make that request elsewhere.
4. You can tell that person that you don't feel you are important enough to be on her Profile and that perhaps someone with

more rank or personal experience with the requester could be more helpful to her, effectively saying, "It's not you, it's me."

Chapter 7 Summary

- When navigating through your network on LinkedIn, it is important to treat each interaction with open-mindedness. Had I focused the content of my meeting with Jeff Bussgang on just being introduced to my target in his network, I would have missed out on building a great client and business partner relationship.
- A warm introduction is no replacement for competence. It will usually get you one meeting with your target market, but after that it is up to your professional value proposition to earn an invitation to return.
- It is helpful to recognize that, for you, certain points in time are better than others for building social capital with someone. One such example is giving public recognition to those whom you feel deserve it, especially when you are speaking in front of a relevant audience.
- When requesting Recommendations, consider that endorsements should be from people whose name or position resonates with your target market and/or people who have something compelling to say about you. The stronger these two elements become, the more impact the Recommendation will have.
- When providing Recommendations for others, it will save you time to ask the requester to draft up a Recommendation for you to edit, reflecting some details of your relationship.

8

Make Better Introductions

As I sought to help the world adopt LinkedIn in a massively scalable way, I knew I had a long task list in order to compel large corporate clients—not to mention LinkedIn itself—to embrace my company and my plans. One key item on that list was to demonstrate expertise in social technologies beyond LinkedIn so that we could converse intelligently about LinkedIn's comparative value. And it would be even better if that expertise could be publicly recognized by someone who had a position of esteem in our target market.

I met and earned the respect of one such key influencer when I set my sights on Scott Kirsner soon after I had settled into Cambridge. Scott is widely known for informing and influencing his readers with his *Innovation Economy* blog and *Boston Globe* column. I had heard his name often throughout my business dealings when I first arrived in Kendall Square and thought he was someone I would want to know.

At this point, I knew if people began to get on board with LinkedIn, it could alter the way the world does business. If I could get in touch with Scott, I could potentially gain valuable feedback about my LinkedIn skills from a knowledgeable and well-connected personality in Boston. I was hoping to have our brand projected to people in the area in a much broader way than what I was already doing (as it would be if Scott chose to comment favorably about me in any of his writings). As it turns out, I was able to do both.

How, you ask, did I get in front of Scott Kirsner long enough for him to tell the greater Boston area that I know LinkedIn and, more specifically, that I was able to teach an early LinkedIn employee of an even greater value within the platform?

Well, my first step was to follow Scott on a regular basis (10 years ago this was considered stalking; now Twitter has made it acceptable). I learned about him and his interests through his blog and tweets. One specific tweet piqued my interest about Scott's mention of a networking breakfast that would precede one of the Future Forward events he moderates every year. Future Forward hosts area chief investment officers (CIOs), chief technical officers (CTOs), entrepreneurs, and investors for a once a year get-together to discuss innovative technologies. Not only would the event help me learn about the community; it could also allow me to meet many people who might influence my business.

My research on Scott prepared me to:

- Discuss topics that were relevant and interesting to him (via Twitter and his other public commentary).
- Mention mutual connections in our networks (via LinkedIn).
- Offer to give him a free LinkedIn consultation in return for his highly regarded and constructive criticism (a real call to action).
- Give him compelling reasons to evaluate me and then mention his evaluation to his audience (providing quality content).

So I went to the breakfast. I arrived at the event early, thinking that if Scott was hosting, he'd be there early as well, and he was. I struck up a conversation in the least harassing way possible by talking about things he'd written, making sure to insert our mutual connections into the brief conversation:

"I noticed via LinkedIn that you know Tim Rowe and Jeff Bussgang [mutual contacts I shared with Scott and well-respected professionals in the community]; how do you know them?" As a side note, I didn't contact Tim or Jeff before bringing up their names to Scott, but I made sure that the two people I mentioned were people I knew well enough and was confident would speak favorably of me if Scott went back and checked with them. Building strong and credible relationships with people like this will allow you to use (not abuse) your relations with them, knowing that they will have only good things to say when your name comes up in conversation.

Those names, also well-respected by Scott, seemed to help keep his interest and we continued chatting until the Future Forward program began. After sitting through an informative session on term sheets at the law firm where the event was held, I caught up with Scott as he was walking out the door with just enough time to explain my proposition. I told him that I believed what I was doing with LinkedIn was revolutionary and that, left alone, people just weren't adopting it fast enough. In the last moments of our conversation, I offered him a free LinkedIn session. Scott was intrigued, in part by what I was doing with LinkedIn and, I think, in part by my persistence. He agreed to meet me again.

Scott joined me for a two-hour LinkedIn consultation at my office. I was curious as to the content of the volumes of notes he was scribbling down, as well as what he was going to do with the information. Did he agree with what I was saying? Or was he writing about how much of a fool I was for spending so much time on LinkedIn when other newer, more "exciting" platforms were available to me?

After our meeting, Scott reached out to Lee Hower (one of LinkedIn's early employees, mentioned in Chapter 4), whom I had met a few weeks before. My two interactions with Scott, coupled with the apparently confirming discussion he had with Lee, resulted in an article on the front page of the *Boston Globe* business section titled "Make Better Introductions." And from that point on, I held the moniker of the "LinkedIn Jedi," which, as you can imagine, was good for business. Going back to Twitter, one of those initial tools I used to find and decide I wanted to convey my value proposition to Scott, you can see his tweet about this article on the day it came out:

> @ScottKirsner: *Today's Globe column, full of advice on how to become a LinkedIn power user, is #1 on the most-emailed-stories list:* http://bit.ly/18Y6Dj

7:09 PM *September 6, 2009*

This first *joint forces* mission of my civilian career had to do with several key "allies": Twitter, LinkedIn, quality content, and a good, old-fashioned, in-person call to action at a networking event. This tangible business success illustrates the strength of relationships that can be harnessed as a result of integrated Linked-In usage at the personal level. Living overseas before moving to the United States, I had only a small network in Boston, yet I had swiftly gained access to a highly influential figure using multiple tools to which you also have access, not to mention the fact that soon afterward, I was given greater exposure to all of Boston and beyond, online and in print.

With my rapidly growing network and client list, positive press in a well-known source like the *Boston Globe,* and the continuous reinforcing interactions confirming that our approach to LinkedIn was unique and altering business, I set my sights back toward LinkedIn itself.

Finally Seeing the Mountain View

My efforts toward building a distinguished network resulted in countless opened doors, but I still saw a greater opportunity to leverage my LinkedIn talents and decided that I needed LinkedIn's brand behind me to fully realize it. The general population just wasn't naturally and rapidly adopting the nonintuitive nature of how to best use LinkedIn's business intelligence in the real world, and I saw significant opportunities to tailor and deliver our methods to corporations.

In some ways, LinkedIn was similar to Microsoft Excel at the time: Although many consider Excel to be a widely used tool, the majority of its users only employ a fraction of its capabilities. In the same way that most people have never used What-If Analysis or recorded macros in Excel, most don't have strategies for their automated people or company searches or for LinkedIn. The challenge LinkedIn faced was getting the world to use its platform at a higher level of comfort and proficiency despite the other, *flashier* social networks available for use. Its users needed to appreciate the value of investing their time and money into upgrading Profiles, connecting with people they already know, posting jobs, and exploring how much utility they can get out of their networks. I believed I could help.

I created a solution to this challenge called *LinkedIn Boot Camp*, the first of four business plans I formed to leverage my expertise in LinkedIn. This program played on my military background and was designed to deliver LinkedIn directly to the conference rooms, boardrooms, and classrooms of the organizations in the platform's target market, powered by my marketing firm as a joint venture with LinkedIn. Our team members would train and interact with all those professionals who, at that time, thought, "I get business through relationships, *not* online."

The most difficult part of presenting *LinkedIn Boot Camp* would be to prove that our offering was unique and that I was not just another social media trainer amongst a sea of thousands. A key point of differentiation was my strategic vision for the platform: first enabling each individual to more efficiently and comfortably use (and not abuse) his network; then giving the individual incentive to use his network synergistically with his coworkers for mutual benefit to himself and his company. I wanted to convey this differentiator to influential team members at LinkedIn in order to earn their official brand approval, thereby enabling us to spread the word more broadly about the value we provided.

I was invited to present our boot camp idea to LinkedIn's senior products team at the company's Mountain View (California) headquarters. This invitation came not through LinkedIn but through a good old-fashioned introduction from Dan Allred, a senior relationship manager at Silicon Valley Bank. Dan saw the value behind what we were doing with LinkedIn, even before we met in person. In our first phone conversation, I convinced Dan that the track we were on was undeniably the right one. He suggested I reach out to his contact, Jeff Glass (the managing director from Bain Capital Ventures discussed in Chapter 2), who was also a LinkedIn board observer.

A Couple for the Books

One of my most notable (and favorite) personal LinkedIn consulting sessions was with one of Dan Allred's colleagues, a man named Oscar Jazdowski, who was a senior relationship manager at Silicon Valley Bank (SVB). The fact that he had a bucket of beers and a pizza waiting when I got to his office may have helped. Since then, Oscar and Dan have introduced me to many of their colleagues and, consequently, SVB has grown to become an excellent client of Clearly Creative and RockTech. SVB understood that networking isn't about being nice to people so that you can start selling to them; it's about building relationships, beginning with the first meeting.

My experience with Oscar served as a microcosm of the way SVB does business, something that became most apparent to me when I was hired to take SVB's clients through LinkedIn at their venture capitalist (VC) Summit in Utah in July 2010. I received clear guidance from their leadership to help these VC chief financial officers (CFOs) make LinkedIn work for each of them first, and then their respective firms. It is, after all, a tool that allows individuals to stimulate a direct and warm introduction to the decision maker of a target company—if used properly.

It was at this VC Summit where I spent 90 minutes with one of the four small groups I trained. I finished by asking if anyone in the room felt that LinkedIn could not work for them immediately in a tangible fashion. One vice president and CFO, Jane NotForMe, raised her hand and said, "CIOs at the LPs (limited partners) I'm targeting aren't using LinkedIn, so no—I don't think this can work for me."

To address her concern, I proposed that we log into Jane's Profile (which had approximately 100 connections already—a respectable number) to see if she was correct. We performed a tailored search for chief investment officers (CIOs) in industries of organizations that could potentially be LPs for her firm. After I made two tweaks to that initial search, she saw the name of a CIO she wanted to get to adjacent to the name of someone she apparently knew very well who could introduce her to said CIO, and she was convinced. This clarified for her that LinkedIn is not always easy to appreciate conceptually; it is much more helpful to experience its power in the context of your own network as its value can sound a bit too good to be true.

Utilizing the intelligence-gathering process I conduct before meeting new people, I saw via LinkedIn that Jeff Glass was connected to Tim Rowe. Tim is the founder and CEO of the Cambridge Innovation Center (CIC) where Clearly Creative held office space. In my note to Jeff, I suggested that we meet at CIC, fully understanding that coming to our building could potentially be appealing to him if he knew Tim and the CIC. Hanging out in the heart of Kendall Square, where some of the fastest-growing technology and life sciences companies are located, is not exactly a bad way for a VC like Jeff to spend his time.

Jeff agreed to meet me, and at that meeting we casually discussed topics ranging from the business benefits of LinkedIn to the potential market for a civilian Ranger School. After this first meeting, I believed that Jeff saw me as a LinkedIn zealot; however, I knew he needed to be convinced a bit further that I was truly unique. Later that year, just before I left for a speaking engagement at the National Venture Capital Association (NVCA) conference in

November of 2009, I contacted Jeff, determined to show him why our use of LinkedIn was so distinct from the rest of the pack.

I walked him through some of the more Advanced LinkedIn usage that has changed the minds of so many nonbelievers regarding the platform's value, including just how our clients were actually increasing their revenues. Jeff figured out during that call that I was doing much more than other social media trainers to whom he'd been exposed and he immediately introduced me to Deep Nishar. In an e-mail introducing us, Jeff presented me as an entrepreneur who knew LinkedIn well enough to teach him (a participant in the $53 million investment round of funding that LinkedIn had recently raised) new and valuable things about using LinkedIn's product.[1] He cited Deep as the brilliant former Google phenom who was going to help take LinkedIn to the next level. Shortly after Jeff risked some social capital with Deep by suggesting that he meet me, Deep invited me to meet with him and his products team at LinkedIn's headquarters in Mountain View.

Three weeks later I found myself walking through LinkedIn's front door. I was ready to propose *LinkedIn Boot Camp* to the products team, knowing that Deep's support could provide me the LinkedIn brand, which I thought was what I needed at that time to succeed. I entered that meeting expecting that my ability to help teach the world about LinkedIn was about to be reinforced by LinkedIn itself.

When we sat down to discuss my proposal, he listened thoughtfully, asked several questions, and expressed his feedback that my original idea wasn't scalable enough for him. He was also curious to know why I felt I needed LinkedIn's permission to implement the program. Deep explained that at Google, he had witnessed many companies profitably capitalizing on the search engine's technology by selling search engine optimization (SEO) and search engine marketing (SEM) training and services. Once I told Deep that I wanted to use the LinkedIn brand to make this a successful and scalable operation that cut through the noise in the social media training space, he understood that *LinkedIn Boot*

Camp wasn't something I could effectively do alone. He then listed a few reasons surrounding my first business plan that didn't fully resonate with him before departing for another meeting. He left me with 30 minutes to spare before I would be meeting again with him, but also with his most senior products team to discuss how we could potentially work with LinkedIn.

So I had received clear feedback from one of LinkedIn's top executives that he was interested in the goal I was trying to achieve but that my execution plan wasn't strong enough for him . . . *yet*. I got to work revamping, revising, and reevaluating my plan based on the input I had just received. For those 30 minutes, my focus became winning over Deep and his products posse in order to get to next steps with what would become my second LinkedIn-infused business plan.

I used each of those 1,800 seconds to overhaul my plan in a manner that I expected would get Deep's team to understand my value proposition and back me with their brand. What emerged from the cafeteria that August morning would eventually become known as the Certified LinkedIn Instructor Program (CLIP).

I walked into the meeting with a redesign to my original proposal. Deep gave me a 30-second introduction, telling his team that I had a successful marketing firm in Boston and that I came highly recommended by Jeff Glass. At the mention of the social capital that Jeff had provided to put me in that room, I saw interest sparking from some members of the group. Various elements of my proposal seemed to have intrigued them and prompted questions involving everything from the LinkedIn changes I would recommend and the kind of training that I would implement to how my ideas emerged and evolved. But something became clear to me during the session: they looked as if they were mid-campaign in a multifront war. The brilliant minds in that room had already generated the functional improvements to LinkedIn's platform that I knew all too well. And, as I was about to see, they were rolling out major changes to the platform shortly after that meeting, which would keep them busy for quite a while—foreshadowing their initial response to my request for their brand.

It wasn't long after returning to Boston that we revised, refined, and sent the CLIP proposal to LinkedIn, and the answer came soon afterward: CLIP was just not a priority for LinkedIn at the time. What I was doing was no simple venture, and they didn't find my proposition compelling or scalable enough to displace any of their priorities at the time. They were adding about a million users to their platform every two weeks, while improving the product: an undertaking that was tantamount to building a plane while in flight, adding new engines, crew, and passengers at the same time. What I wouldn't know for another few months was that LinkedIn was about to launch its partnership with Twitter and Microsoft, open its application programming interface (API) and unveil even more new features, raising the bar for me to provide a resonating and scalable solution to train their target market.

LinkedIn's response didn't negate what I still recognized as a significant business opportunity: bringing LinkedIn to the world in terms that the world could understand. I used this experience to bring to my board and advisors a new consideration: how to leverage our expertise in a manner that would eventually earn LinkedIn's brand but that could gain momentum without it? And yet again, my network took care of me.

I soon found another ally in a fairly well-connected New Yorker, Mark Rockefeller, who brought in the reinforcements.

Chapter 8 Summary

- I met Scott Kirsner and received great press as a result of a combination of tools including Twitter, LinkedIn, quality content, and a networking event. This effort demonstrates the importance of utilizing various online and offline tools for business and communication in order to be successful in your endeavors.
- Another way to build social capital with others is by being appropriately persistent. Listening to people who evaluate you, digesting their feedback, and proposing a thoughtful new idea helps build strong relationships fast.

9

In Like a Ranger, Out Like a Rockefeller

So THERE I was, in an elevator heading up to the fifty-sixth floor of New York City's 30 Rockefeller Plaza (also known as *30 Rock*) to deliver a presentation on how LinkedIn was going to change business as well as the role my company could play in delivering technologies like LinkedIn to a market that needed it. There was a major opportunity to leverage LinkedIn—in addition to countless other technologies—with the would-be partners I was about to meet. Given all that occurred to get me to this situation, I started to feel somewhat reflective as I sped upward in the GE building's elevator that day.

Although countless individuals had helped me get to where I was at that point, one advisor, influencer, and friend was salient— and not just because he happened to be standing next to me. That man was Scott McCabe. I did not meet Scott through LinkedIn, or even through traditional methods of networking. In fact, the way in which I met Mr. McCabe is worth a bit of ink to explain.

Working Out the Kinks in My Network

After attending a military out-processing seminar in my last year on active duty, I approached one of the panelists (we'll call him

John Civilitary) in order to discuss how to morph army Dave into civilian Dave. One element of this plan included building a personal board of advisors by going to a gym located in Boston's financial district at 5 A.M. on a daily basis. I explained that I thought this would allow me to meet three goals simultaneously: staying in shape, demonstrating to potential employers or advisors that I could handle long hours on my new job, and setting up the chance to network with like-minded folks. Civilitary informed me, politely yet condescendingly, that people don't want to network at 5 A.M. in a gym; they just want to work out. He suggested that I instead attend some networking events in the city's financial district after work to accomplish my goals. I now realize that through my flippant use of the word *networking*, I mistakenly conveyed that I was going to show up at the gym with a mocha frappe latte in one hand and a pile of business cards in the other. My words led him to believe I would be setting up shop in the locker room to pass out my résumé and/or business plan to anyone who would listen. That's not quite what I had in mind.

Evident from this interaction is that traditionally, networking has been done a certain way—and people have found success with it, and thus continued to network that way, despite the rapid evolution of new and better ways to meet people.

In many cases, when you're where you want to be, doing what you want to do, you're more likely to find people like yourself with whom you'd like to work. And at the very least, you'll enjoy what you're doing (instead of traveling to and hanging out at a venue after a long day at work with a pocketful of business cards hoping this time—not spent with your family or friends in a social capacity—is worth it). For me, this meant spending time at the gym.

I put myself in a situation where I would meet like-minded people in a way that we could informally evaluate one another. I went to the gym, worked out, and left; but I did so in ways that facilitated my goal of quickly building solid relationships. When I went to the gym, I accomplished a goal of having a good workout, regardless of whether I found my next job, a new client, or a new business partner. However, I made it a point to never wear head-phones while working out alongside these potential advisors, friends, or business partners. I knew I wouldn't be approachable if I was in my own world. And because I didn't want to be *that guy* networking in the gym, I felt it was better to be approached than to approach others.

One morning while at the gym, I had just finished my workout and was in line at the water fountain. Scott turned around after getting a drink, looked at the crimson lettering on my shirt, and said, "You go to Harvard?" The ice was broken when I replied, "Yeah, I'm getting my master's there now. You?" We chatted briefly, then parted ways and called it a day.

Note that in this case I took a more passive approach to net-working instead of being overzealous or pushy. It was easy for me to do so because I was in a place where networking was only part of my goal. I subtly tossed out a conversation piece without saying a word. I consciously wore T-shirts while working out that dis-played a brand relevant to me that would relate to people with whom I'd share a similar background. The attire provided a subtle icebreaker for Scott or anyone else who felt interested in speaking with me. This could also manifest itself as a lapel pin on a suit or a charity bracelet (such as the yellow LIVESTRONG® wristband) in more traditional business settings.

Little did I know just how significant Scott would be to my fu-ture as a close friend and business partner. When I filled him in on Clearly Creative and my ambitions, he repeatedly invited me to his office to be the advisor/sounding board that I sought. He then made many fruitful introductions for me to clients, employees, and strategic business partners, which ultimately led to my meeting Mark Rockefeller.

Now, fast-forward to early 2010. Scott and I were riding the elevator to meet Mark Rockefeller and several of his business part-ners. I went into this meeting expecting that this could be a make-or-break moment for me, and just might dictate how far my LinkedIn expertise would take me. If I succeeded in convincing this group of professionals that I was on to something big, the resultant partnership could be powerful. It could give me the edge I needed to bring our LinkedIn methodology to the world, associated with a brand already resonant with my target market, without having to wait for the formal relationship with LinkedIn (that would come later). Mark immediately showed interest in our plan. But when he asked about my support of the Wounded Warrior Project (a nonprofit organization that empowers injured soldiers returning from military service in Iraq and Afghanistan), he cemented my belief that he represented a relationship worth growing. In fact, it was this *peripheral* nonprofit element of our interactions that helped deepen our professional relationship much more quickly than anything else. This is a great example where, in building long-lasting relationships, it's important to work with people whom you believe you can trust. More often than not, the people I trust most are those with a strong nonprofit or otherwise selfless component to their value system, or at least those seeking to find one. This personality differentiator may manifest itself in how a person conducts themselves in their family life, a charity, the military, and so on. Knowing that people aren't only seeking to make money and that they care about some bigger picture may be a useful sign that you want to find a way to collaborate.

It was during that meeting in 30 Rock that we decided as a group there was too much potential energy in the room for us not to explore doing something together. I made the parallel to Mark that much like his great-grandfather who didn't invent oil but found the best way to bring it to market, we were taking a similar approach with delivering new technologies to market as they sprung up like oil fields did in the 1900s. We churned out the third business plan I explored surrounding use of my LinkedIn prowess in conjunction with the Rockefeller brand. This idea was one that had been much more consultative in nature (and therefore less scalable) than I, or LinkedIn, was seeking. It was only after months of discussions with more investors, clients, and business partners that we realized business plan #3 just was not yet the right fit. That is when RockTech was born, and we had the idea to create what would eventually become known as the Technology Adoption

Platform (TAP) for LinkedIn, which allowed us to deliver our LinkedIn methodology much more effectively than anyone before us to positively impact more people in a highly measurable fashion.

Social Capital in Leadership: A Real Tearjerker

Embarking upon a business plan with some new partners caused me to think about the leadership I would have to provide as the opportunity and team continued to grow. In terms of social capital, your leadership style can provide many opportunities to generate (or burn) it. While serving in the ROTC program, I had the privilege of helping some of our country's most talented cadets to identify if and how they could lead troops in a combat environment. The first three years of most cadets' ROTC experiences culminates in the Leadership Development and Assessment Course (LDAC). LDAC is a rigorous eight-week training program where thousands of cadets from around the country travel to Fort Lewis, Washington, to be trained and coached by ROTC evaluators. During my first summer teaching the program, I was one such LDAC evaluator and found a unique way to build some social capital with my troops.

For the eight weeks I was assigned to my platoon of about 60 cadets (which was made up of four squads of 15 cadets each), my general responsibilities included overseeing and ensuring safe and effective cadet-led training while mentoring and evaluating three cadets each day during their rotating leadership positions. I evaluated their overall leadership ability, including their character, command presence, and intellectual capacity to lead others while enduring stress. Effective leadership, of course, is not all about barking orders and expecting others to follow them. Much of leadership has to do with earning respect, and often social capital, with your

(continued)

(*continued*)

subordinates so that they operate in compliance with your intentions, especially when nobody is looking over their shoulders. This is one of the softer sides of leader development that I wanted my cadets to learn.

During LDAC, one of the training exercises that cadets must accomplish includes entering a chamber filled with tear gas (the same gas that is used by law enforcement officers to disband rioters). Cadets enter the chamber wearing their protective mask (pro-mask) and then remove it while they are inside to inhale the debilitating fumes. Tear gas causes intense burning of the eyes, nose, throat, and skin, commonly including violent nausea and physical incapacitation. That is why it is effective at dispersing unruly crowds, and not something you generally want to be exposed to in a small non-ventilated building . . . such as a gas chamber.

This exercise builds each cadet's confidence in his equipment, showing him that his pro-mask works well when used properly. It also prepares him for the potential of being exposed to tear gas while in combat so he knows how his body will react when exposed. To some cadets, this is exciting. To some, it is horrifying. Either way, the gas chamber generally elicits some form of significant emotional response in those preparing to enter it.

One of the key elements of being a leader is to lead by example. As the overall leader of my platoon of cadets, I was required to perform much paperwork and logistics coordination but had the freedom to participate in any training exercise I desired. Although not the most "fun" exercise (we also trained via zip lines over water, obstacle courses, grenade throwing, and other events civilians pay high fees to conduct), I recognized that positive and negative anticipation was growing around our "gas chamber day" and a good leadership lesson was at hand.

On the day my platoon went through the gas chamber, I wanted to lead by example and demonstrate how to build social capital with my cadets who knew I was not required to expose myself to the gas chamber. To do so, I first entered the chamber before my lead squad of cadets without wearing my pro-mask. I stayed in as long as I could bear it and came out with my red eyes tearing, my sore throat coughing, and demonstrating other nonglamorous results of the chamber. After a few moments of regaining my composure, I started laughing and joking about the experience with that initial squad, building confidence in them that they would survive when it was their turn to do the same. The squad then entered the chamber wearing their pro-masks. After a few minutes I followed them in, again, without my pro-mask. Having seen me just go through it once already, all the pro-mask-covered faces turned to me in unison as I entered the shack for a second time. I ran throughout the chamber for as long as I could bear it, making jokes and high-fiving each cadet before telling them I'd see them outside as the burning intensified and reduced my ability to continue speaking. I then repeated this maskless exercise for the following three squads as well.

Afterward I felt like a worn-out shoe having been gassed five times in 90 minutes. However, with hydration and lunch, I was almost as good as new by the afternoon and went on with my duties. Later that night, one of my more timid cadets came up to me and said, "Sir, I was petrified of the gas chamber. But when you walked in with no mask, it made me confident and even excited about this training event, and I knew I'd be fine. If you could do it five times and laugh about it, I'd survive. I can't thank you enough."

That cadet's words, and similar statements from others, reinforced to me the value of building social capital with those whom you already may have legal or corporate authority to tell what to do. For those employees or employers reading

(continued)

> (*continued*)
> this, especially those who think you have subordinates or peers around you who don't seem motivated to always do what you would like them to, consider "nontraditional" methods of building social capital with them. In this example, I listened to the pain points of my cadets and recognized I could do something that was "outside the box," at my own expense, to alleviate their pain points while also setting a good example. What types of "gas" can you ingest to build social capital with your coworkers?

Although TAP ultimately became a tool that overlays and integrates into just about any underutilized software platform to speed up, track, and influence adoption, it all started with LinkedIn. The content in *TAP for LinkedIn* initially helps users learn LinkedIn using our "4P" methodology:

1. Privacy and security protection
2. Profile improvement
3. Proper network growth
4. Proactive business tool usage

So, on that note, enough about me; let's get technical.

Chapter 9 Summary

- Networking can be an unpleasant experience if not done thoughtfully. Finding a way to combine your personal and professional interests into a recurring item on your schedule often makes networking more effective and enjoyable.
- My relationships with some of my most strategically impactful business partners grew first from other strong relationships with people who felt it relevant to introduce us. These relationships often grew deeper from multiple levels of shared personal and professional interests.

■ A common denominator in some of my strongest relationships has been an element of selfless service or support of
a nonprofit organization. I've seen this take many forms:
people who regularly build social capital with those around
them without ever seeking to use it, veterans who have de-
ployed to combat zones without complaint, donors to my
nonprofit initiatives, and many others.

■ Our core methodology in adopting LinkedIn surrounds a "4P"
approach:
  ○ Privacy and security protection
  ○ Profile improvement
  ○ Proper network growth
  ○ Proactive business tool usage

PART

3

Getting Technical

10

Disrupting Your Privacy and Security

As THE FIRST step in our "4P" methodology, *protection* is a great place to start building your LinkedIn expertise. User concerns about privacy and security are some of the more common reasons people cite for not using LinkedIn or other valuable social platforms. Users don't harness their networks' potential, because they're hesitant to give away what they feel is too much information about themselves or their connections. Some are concerned with being spammed, harassed, or having their network information sold by companies that abuse professionals' data to sell leads to their clients. It's therefore essential to alleviate these fears before moving on to profile refinement, network growth, or using LinkedIn's business tools. So in order to fully understand and overcome some of the major concerns you may have, I'll first share an explanation of why LinkedIn is a *disruptive technology*, which can ease the potential fears you may have about the tool.

A Disruptive Technology

Many people are reluctant to use LinkedIn to manage, grow, or reach out to their networks because it is a disruptive technology.

I adopted this phrase from Harvard Business School Professor Clay Christensen, who coined and popularized this theory (in addition to achieving many other notable accomplishments).[1] Christensen has since tweaked and expanded the definition, but my adaptation of his lesson with respect to LinkedIn is as follows:

Throughout history, there have been various disruptors that have challenged societies to rethink the way they conduct themselves; the telephone, personal computers, and e-mail are three examples. The term *disruptor* comes from the subsequent displacement of a previous innovation, which causes lovers of the status quo to be hesitant to accept them. For instance, it took years for people to accept the telephone over the tele- graph, the personal computer over a nonelectronic workstation, and e-mail over handwritten correspondence. It takes time to fully adopt these disruptors into society, yet once they are inte- grated into personal and ultimately collective behaviors, they create significant leaps in efficiency. The outcome is worth the initial investment of learning a new tool, or as they say in the military, "No pain, no gain."

LinkedIn is a disruptor but not in the way that most people think. This tool is not displacing human interaction, which is a common misperception held by people who have achieved great success without using online tools thus far. These skeptics are missing the key fact that what LinkedIn (and other disruptive technologies) is displacing isn't going to be missed.

To zero in on what *is* being displaced by LinkedIn, consider these questions: Have you ever made a cold call to stimulate business? Or sat through a job interview with a company you decided you didn't want to work for after meeting the inter- viewer, maybe even after multiple interviews? Have you searched long and hard for talent that is the right fit for a posi- tion? Have you stood at the threshold of a major deal and had a team scour the Internet for business intelligence on someone sitting across from you at the negotiation table but came up with nothing of significant use? Have you spent countless hours at networking events, hoping that of the handful of people you met, at least one would become a lead, a deal, a job—or at the very least someone who has something half-interesting to say?

Most of us have experienced at least some of these frustrations, if not all of them, and these types of interactions unveil what LinkedIn is disrupting in all these situations: *wasting time.*

LinkedIn is displacing our current methods of wasting time— methods we've come to accept as a necessary cost of doing business today. Yet there is a great deal of inefficiency in the way we generate leads, hire, research, and network in general. By replacing those currently accepted inefficient behaviors with more effective and more enjoyable tactics, LinkedIn streamlines the critical processes needed to achieve our business goals. When used correctly, this tool allows us to dramatically reduce the time it takes to meet the people we seek based on information that has never been available to us before. LinkedIn provides the personalized social mapping ability that indicates the relationship paths to those professionals we seek, or those from whom we should steer clear.

This argument also supports the theory that LinkedIn is years ahead of its time. Many successful professionals are still getting comfortable with online social networking, yet simply understanding how to use these tools isn't what brings users success. To really leverage the power of LinkedIn, there must be a significant change in people's long-term behavior. It is human nature to resist improvements to some of our most commonly accepted behaviors, despite our acceptance that we *should* do it.

Some people are reluctant to upload their contacts' e-mail addresses into LinkedIn to find people they know who are already using LinkedIn. Generally it's a managing partner, CFO, board member, or other leader who has spent most of their distinguished career building and nurturing relationships offline that shares this concern. If you agree with these naysayers, I ask you this: Do you put your financial information on the Internet either to make purchases or for online banking? Isn't the knowledge of your professional connections equally as sensitive as knowledge of your financial transactions (especially since you're not actually putting sensitive network information into cyberspace via LinkedIn, but instead only relaying the fact that you *have* that information to those in your network)?

Also effective at disarming the argument against exposing such protected information about your contacts to LinkedIn is the fact that the vast majority of personal e-mails are sent over the unsecured Internet on a regular basis. Concerned about your contacts' e-mail addresses being blasted into the web unsecured? Well, you're probably doing this dozens (if not hundreds) of times a day already.

It's critical that we discuss privacy and security before moving on to the meat of LinkedIn's valuable features to ensure that everyone using the site feels comfortable enough to use it effectively. You may feel more secure with LinkedIn and realize it represents minimal risk when you learn that Reid Hoffman was also on the board of directors of PayPal when it was founded.[2] I think you'll agree that this financial transaction platform, which enables peer-to-peer monetary deals to occur online, would not be too appealing without proper security measures. When eBay bought PayPal in 2002, Hoffman received his share of the exit proceeds and used that wealth to found and invest in LinkedIn. Having a founder with such a background—one who cut his teeth in a business that conducts financial transactions online—has clearly rooted privacy and security considerations into LinkedIn's DNA.

Perhaps not so ironically, the underlying nature of LinkedIn is to permit the peer-to-peer transactions of the rapidly growing social capital trade and to connect professionals in the least intrusive way possible. So if it's easier for you, think of LinkedIn as PayPal for your social capital.

Privacy and Security Best Practices

There are several privacy and security measures available to LinkedIn users that many of our clients consistently deem valuable. Some of these are featured in the material that follows,

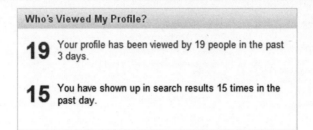

Figure 10.1 Seeing Who Has Viewed Your Profile

and are all located in your "Settings," which is at the top right of every LinkedIn page. There are many more privacy and security settings that we regularly consider when building personal and corporate strategies, but considering the following tips should help most readers rest assured that LinkedIn isn't going to abuse their contacts or harass their network:

Profile Viewing Privacy: One feature that generates a lot of interest from users governs Profile viewing privacy. You can use Facebook to regularly check in on your old college flame, and she'll never know. On the other hand, in LinkedIn, the default setting for your account is to allow people whose Profiles you've visited to see some information about you. If you scroll down on the right side of your home page, you will see a section titled, "Who's Viewed My Profile?" as shown in Figure 10.1.

To choose what people see about you after you've viewed their Profiles, click on the Settings link shown in Figure 10.2.

LinkedIn then brings you to the screen shown in Figure 10.3, where you can select the following item, circled in this figure: select what others see when you've viewed their Profile.

The screen pictured in Figure 10.4 displays the three options you are then given.

Figure 10.2 Selecting the Settings Link

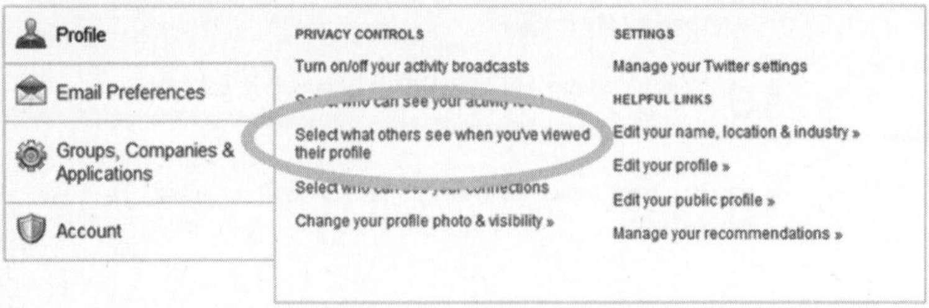

Figure 10.3   Selecting What Others See When You've Viewed Their Profiles

If you never touch this section, the default setting is the middle anonymous option, shown in Figure 10.4. Upon hearing this fact, most people immediately click the third option, thinking, "I don't want people to know that I'm looking at their profile; they'll think I'm stalking them!"

There *are* a few things to consider before you dive into stealth mode. First, wouldn't you feel somewhat flattered if you saw that someone was looking at your Profile? Not only can viewing someone's page be considered a subtle form of flattery and contact,

Figure 10.4   Choosing What Others See When You've Viewed Their Profiles

it can also encourage that person to click on your Profile to view the message you project, potentially driving more traffic to your Profile or company website. After all, you took the time to input valuable information about yourself and your organization into what is becoming the public Profile of record for professionals' information on the web (as per our discussion on Google from Chapter 2). Why not showcase it? I often recommend that most people, if comfortable doing so, go into what I call "full disclosure," by showing their name and headline while viewing others' Profiles. However, if this is going to keep you from using the tool effectively, then by all means, hunker down into stealth mode. It's far more important for you to feel comfortable using LinkedIn (it is then more likely that you will use LinkedIn more often). And for those who are unsure about being out in the open, you'll be comforted to know that according to LinkedIn, "You will never (not even with a premium subscription upgrade) receive more in-depth information about a viewer if they have chosen to hide their identity in their Privacy Settings."[3] Notably, what you project impacts what you can see about viewing your Profile. Unless you are in full "disclosure" or you upgrade to a premium LinkedIn account, you will be unable to see who has viewed your Profile.

Sharing your connections list: The ability to control who can see your connections list provides comfort to many professionals when using LinkedIn. Those who hesitate to reveal their networks for fear of having them poached by competitors use this feature to mitigate this concern. You have two simple options with this section: keep your list of connections to yourself, or share it with all your 1st degree connections. It's important to note that the only way anyone can see this comprehensive list of the people to whom you are connected is if you invite (and they accept) or you accept an invitation from that person first. This is where you can allow those 1st degree connections to see the rest of your 1st degree connections or hide the list from them. Keep in mind that no one to whom you are connected ever has access to the contact information of your other 1st degree connections, even if you choose to show your connections list. In this case, they will only have access to the names of

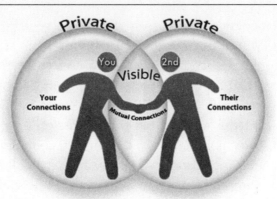

Figure 10.5　Infographic of Mutual Connections

Figure credit: Katie Berdan

the other people with whom you connect. If you choose to hide your connections list, there are two things to consider:

1. Your 2nd degree connections will still be able to see your mutual connections. For example, let's say that you and John are *not* connected to each other, but that you and John *are* both connected to Jane. This means that John will be able to see that you are one of Jane's connections, and you will be able to see that Jane is one of John's connections, if you and John were to search for each other. See the infographic shown in Figure 10.5 for a clearer picture of this.
2. If you choose to show Recommendations you've received, those who view your Profile will know that you are connected to the recommender: only people you are connected to can recommend you, and anyone in your network can see the Recommendations you choose to display. For example, if I show a Recommendation from Jane, and then John (one of my 3rd degree connections) views my Profile, he will know that I am connected to Jane.

Activity Broadcasts: You have the ability to alert your network when you perform any significant actions within your Profile and have a message (not an e-mail) sent to your

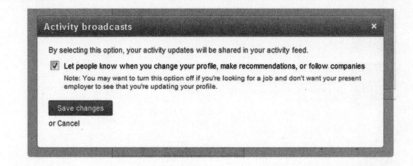

Figure 10.6 Activity Broadcasts

connections' home page news feed, your Company Profile, or your personal Activity Feed. These are called Activity Broadcasts. If you are familiar with Facebook or Twitter, you'll recognize this news feed-like feature that shows you what other people around you are doing. As shown in the Activity Broadcasts screen in Figure 10.6, you can decide whether you want your actions to appear or remain invisible on your connections' Network Activity feeds on their home pages.

To clarify LinkedIn terminology, a Status Update is a conscious message that you choose to write and display on your Profile or project to others (in a way that does not translate into an e-mail for your connections every time you post an update). An example of a Status Update, when viewed from another user's Profile, is shown in Figure 10.7.

Status Updates may appear with other types of Profile updates in the "All Updates" news feed, found on each user's LinkedIn home page (as shown in Figure 10.8). The actual messages you project are based on your Activity Broadcast settings and the frequency with which you generate such messages. We will dive deeper into Status Updates in Chapter 11.

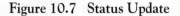

David Gowel Greatest thanks to our troops lost & injured. To ride in or support our Sept. 4th Wounded Warrior cycling event, ask me how you can help.
58 minutes ago · Like · Comment · Send a message · Share

Figure 10.7 Status Update

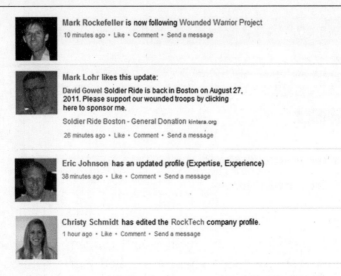

Figure 10.8   Network Feed: Status and Profile Update Examples

Public Profile: Did you know you have the option to show two Profiles (per language) via LinkedIn? There is one that logged-in LinkedIn users can see, and there's one that will show up in Google search results for the nearly 7 billion people on the planet, as long as they can access the Internet. The latter is called your Public Profile, and you have three basic options regarding it:

1. Disable your entire Public Profile.
2. Allow LinkedIn to make everything you put into your Profile visible to the world.
3. Pick and choose what you'd like to show on this public version.

When contemplating your choices for this feature, consider that you take time and effort building your Profile. You've laid out all of the professional information that you want others to know about you; so why would you want to hide that from the world? You know the truth about yourself and your experiences better than anyone. Why not have it come from a credible source?

We generally recommend that you only put information on LinkedIn that you want the world to see (which does not include your personal e-mail address or those of your connections) and then allow everyone to see it. I understand that many people like to keep information about themselves off the Internet, but you should know that train left that station long ago. There are numerous companies that are combing for information online about as many professionals as they can, just so they can repackage it and sell it to business development teams, recruiters, and the like. Which would you prefer to rank higher in search results for your name: the information you authored about yourself or the (potentially erroneous) information about you that may include personal contact information that somehow slipped out?

Invitation Filtering: Under Email Preferences in the Settings section, LinkedIn gives you the option to raise the bar and set limits on the ability of people to send you invitations. For example, if you are a high-profile figure who doesn't want thousands of random people asking to join your network or just a normal discerning professional who doesn't want to waste time sifting through invites, you can control this potential abuse. By clicking Select Who Can Send You Invitations, you have the option to receive:

1. All invitations from anyone on LinkedIn.
2. Only invitations from people who have your e-mail address or are in your imported contacts list.
3. Only invitations from people who appear in your imported contacts (imported contacts are the e-mail addresses that you have uploaded to LinkedIn from your e-mail software—Outlook, Gmail, Yahoo!, or others. There's more information on that in Chapter 12).

Unless this makes you uncomfortable, it is often best to be open to viewing all invitations unless you become negatively impacted by strangers inviting you to join their networks. If someone you don't know asks to be in your network, you always have the option to say no. By clicking Ignore upon receipt of such an invitation, the person won't know whether they were ignored or whether you just haven't viewed their invitation yet. If you are worried about offending others, know that those undesirable invitation senders may assume that you just haven't checked LinkedIn for a while. If you feel someone is sending inappropriate messages, you can select the Report as Spam option, which is your signal to a LinkedIn reviewer to check whether that account should be restricted due to abusive or harassing actions. These are all elements of the self-correcting ecosystem that LinkedIn actively facilitates to keep its users protected.

The actual information you're now armed to protect after reading this section is the topic of our next leg in this LinkedIn journey. Why protect something that's not valuable in the first place? Like most things in business, personal branding requires strategy to do it right. After mastering privacy best practices, you're ready to move on to creating the best Profile for your target market.

Chapter 10 Summary

- Many users don't harness LinkedIn's potential because they're hesitant to give away too much information about themselves or their connections. Alleviating these fears by using the privacy and security controls is essential before you are able to comfortably interact with your network online.
- LinkedIn is a disruptive technology. Throughout history, various disruptors challenged the human race to rethink the way we conduct ourselves (the telephone, personal computers, e-mail, and so on). The term *disruptor* comes from the subsequent displacement of a previous innovation, which causes lovers of the status quo to be hesitant to accept it. LinkedIn is a disruptor, but it is not displacing human interaction, as many have come to think. LinkedIn is displacing the act of *wasting time*.
- LinkedIn was founded and is now led by industry leaders who focus on privacy and security for its users.

11

Projecting the Right Message

LIKE MUCH OF the information on the web, most of the content you provide through your LinkedIn Profile can be seen by many people you do not know. Individuals such as prospective and current clients, business partners, employers, friends, and just about everyone else are finding your LinkedIn Profile via search engines (both inside and outside of LinkedIn). With this Profile in mind, addressing the second "P" in our "4P" methodology, here are two considerations that I suggest keeping at the forefront of your mind as you improve (or create) your LinkedIn Profile: your target market (oddly enough, many people forget about this) and your desired level of professionalism.

Profile Best Practices

A helpful way to explain some best practices is to start at the top and work our way down through specific elements of the LinkedIn Profile:

Name, Headline, Location, Industry: Start by ensuring that each of these four sections is correct and professional. Then ask yourself, "What is going to make my target market want to do

Let Business Find You . . .

One eye-opening experience that showed me how LinkedIn generates incoming marketing opportunities involves Emmy award-winning documentary filmmaker Tim Gray. Although I never met him, I received Tim's invitation to connect in April 2010. Since I follow a litmus test of connecting only with those whom I already know, I was initially inclined to archive Tim's note. But I noticed after quickly looking at his Profile that he included references to the military. I also noticed that he was connected to Kelly Perdew (winner of *The Apprentice 2* and fellow West Point graduate), a trusted connection in my network. Because I had the sense that Tim had collaborative intentions and was connected to someone I also knew and respected, I chose to reply to his invitation. The message was simple, asking how he knew Kelly and probing for his military ties (without initially connecting or giving him my e-mail address).

It turns out that Tim had been attracted to my Profile because it combined both military and marketing elements. The manner in which he replied to my note made me confident that he was someone I'd like to invest time in getting to know, so I asked if he'd like to set up a call to see how we could collaborate. I realized after chatting for a brief period that we had a lot in common. Since he apparently recognized these common links as well, he then introduced me to his friend, Curt Schilling, because of the fantastic support the former Red Sox pitcher was providing for our troops. Because of this unexpected opportunity that I was postured to receive as a result of the way I use LinkedIn, I ended up participating in a Wounded Warrior Project Soldier Ride with Curt and his family less than six months after receiving Tim's initial invitation to connect.[1]

business with me?" One tip that I generally give to our professional clients is to be cautious about putting anything that sounds too much like a marketing slogan or sales pitch into your headline. Since Google (and now the rest of the world) recognizes LinkedIn as a valuable reference source, people are often viewing your Profile to get information about you if they've been introduced to or have otherwise recently met you.

Depending on the target market with whom you are looking to resonate, they may not be looking to read your subjective advertisement about yourself. It's often helpful to stick to the facts up front and then expand on your value proposition in your Summary or Specialties. Of course you know your target market best, so choose the style that you feel will resonate with them.

Picture: Use LinkedIn's sole spot for a photo to insert a professional picture of yourself. Some have disregarded photos, thinking that makes the tool too social. From my experience, it is becoming a sign of completeness: if you don't have one, you don't look as if you are using LinkedIn as well as your competition. You can pull up people on LinkedIn via a mobile device to see their photo if you're meeting them for the first time. This has been particularly helpful for me when meeting people initially, as posting a photo has eliminated the need for me to say ahead of time, "When you arrive, I'll be the guy in the yellow shirt and blond hair whose wife is clearly way out of his league."

Post an Update: Although often dismissed by many professionals as too unprofessional, your Status Update section can do two crucial things if used properly:

1. **It keeps your Profile fresh.** When using your status to share something professional and relevant to your target audience (not, "Hey, I had some tasty pancakes this morning"), a small time stamp is listed next to your comments, which indicates to your viewers how long ago you posted that update. If the status is fresh, people generally assume that the rest of the information on your Profile is up-to-date, which makes them more likely to read what they expect to be current information.

2. **It allows you to send out a subtle message to your 1st degree connections.** Although a Status Update can be seen as similar to Twitter, I generally recommend using these two tools differently because, for most of us, each reaches different target markets. LinkedIn is made up of mutually consenting professionals, whereas Twitter generally allows anyone to follow anyone else. If you are updating your LinkedIn Profile too often with less-than-professional information, perhaps by choosing to duplicate all tweets on LinkedIn, you may turn off your professional connections in LinkedIn who think you are not saying things of interest to them. This could make them turn *you* off from future view in their Network Activity feed by selecting Hide on one of your updates. This will keep you from showing up in their feed unless they release this restriction. If you use this feature appropriately for your target audience, you can send updates to your network that inform them of your events, conference participation, or other relevant happenings that may be interesting to them, and at the very least, keep them from forgetting you. Many people try to accomplish this same goal by sending holiday or birthday correspondence without sincere personalization (think corporate Christmas cards sent to clients without a human signature or personal message). These senders just want others to keep them in mind so their real-world connections will remember them if they need their services or products in the future. That model doesn't scale well; as more individuals gain access to automated Remember Holidays features, we see ourselves getting hundreds of e-cards around these special occasions that don't say anything of significance, negating the feel that anyone actually "remembered" to send you something. Using Status Updates is a much more personal way to keep from being forgotten and can potentially differentiate you from the crowd. Figure 11.1 shows an example of how I've used the tool.

 David Gowel Landing two Blackhawk helicopters at Harvard tomorrow. Let me know if you want to stop by.
12 minutes ago · Like · Comment · Send a message · Share

Figure 11.1   Sample Use of the Status Update Feature

Subtle Constant Contact

While making a major career transition from military to civilian (and while still considering an even bolder leap to entrepreneur), I realized early on that my background made me unique as a newcomer in the marketing industry; so when I had the opportunity to post the Status Update shown in Figure 11.1 on my Profile, I did. This helped me to identify and attract interest from my civilian connections who may have appreciated my military experience.

The seed that grew into this unique event was first planted when I mentioned it to my future boss while interviewing to teach at MIT. I was looking for a good way to not only demonstrate that I could positively engage the community but also demonstrate a "cool factor" of joining the army. After jumping through a series of Olympic-level bureaucratic hoops, our ROTC program orchestrated the landing of two Rhode Island National Guard UH-60 Blackhawk helicopters at Harvard (with many thanks owed to pilot and friend CW4(R) Dick Dube, who introduced me to a bird's-eye view of Fenway Park that day).

Signal: Although not a Profile feature per se, LinkedIn Signal provides a refreshingly simple method of sifting through Status Updates from your connections' Profiles in a time-efficient manner. You can search to find what anyone in a specific company is posting to their LinkedIn Profile. You can search to find what anyone in your network is posting *about* a specific company. You can even search what anyone in a specific city, from a specific company, is posting about *another* company among other variations. While viewing your Profile, Signal search capability is accessible through the menu seen in Figure 11.2.

Current Positions: What do you want to be known for? You may currently be the CFO of a financial services firm as well as a

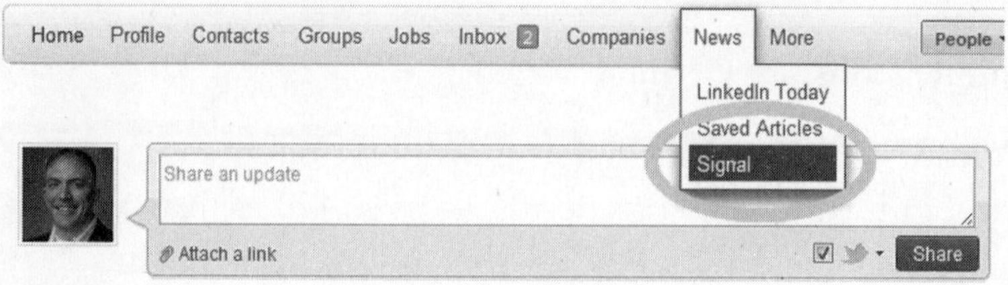

Figure 11.2   How to Find the Signal Feature

board member for a nonprofit and the president of your local chess club. LinkedIn lists your positions chronologically, so you may have to manipulate the dates in order to have what's most relevant to your target market listed first. For integrity purposes, you can explain the correct dates under the description of each position further down in your Profile, as I do in Figure 11.3.

Note: By placing your mouse over the section header in various parts of your LinkedIn Profile, including your Summary, Recommendations, Experience, Certifications, and Education, you can click and drag to reorder these sections. This feature, however, does not currently permit you to reorder your individual positions.

Past Positions: You may want to use the "10-year rule" as a best practice when listing past positions. However, you also may find it helpful to go beyond the past decade to list all your past experiences in LinkedIn (at least briefly) for a couple of reasons:

1. You have the ability to flavor what you do today with everything that you've ever done, even if you've drastically changed industries. I'll use myself as an example, considering you can't get much more opposite than serving in the military

Board Member
East End House ⬈
Nonprofit; Nonprofit Organization Management industry
March 2007 – Present (4 years 3 months)

(Actual Dates: May 2010 to present)
I have the pleasure of working with spectacular board members in support of the extremely competent and caring staff of the East End House: a not-for-profit, multi-service community center and social service agency, established in 1875, with an on-going commitment to a diverse population, providing programs and services to strengthen family and community.

Figure 11.3   Manipulating Dates to Highlight Important Positions

and then becoming a civilian leading a marketing firm (or so you'd think). Recognizing this, but wanting to clarify the value my background provided to my then-current target market, I ended my description for being a platoon leader in Iraq with this statement: "I led my unit to effectively deliver the brand of the U.S. Army to win over the 'hearts and minds' of the civilians, public officials, military and (especially) the insurgents in Iraq." Because of this concise phrase, I've been able to show the relevance from a previous job that most viewers might not have considered apropos without this explanation.

Let's say, for example, that you previously worked in retail but have since moved to accounting. You can tailor the communication and customer interaction skills you learned as a retail manager to the work you will be doing as a CPA, interacting with clients about their private information. If you think long enough, it is likely worth the time for you to bridge the gap for your target market during the brief moments they will view your Profile. If you don't, perhaps nobody will.

2. Listing a past position on LinkedIn gives you the opportunity to search for coworkers who worked at any job at the same time you did. A colleague from your past life (or, more likely, one of their 1st or 2nd degree connections) could have moved into your target market since you last saw him or her. There's a good chance that you would never know of this opportunity unless you've put this past position into LinkedIn. If you are trying to protect your age for fear of discrimination against your experienced nature, you can provide this information for a short period of time, conduct the network growth suggestions mentioned in Chapter 12, and then remove them.

Education: List all relevant education experiences—not just your undergraduate and graduate education—if you think that your target market will find them interesting or differentiating. Are you an accountant who also has a pilot's license? Well, that gives you a distinct value proposition that makes you stand out from the crowd. At the very least, it may give you a conversation piece that can break the ice for new business contacts. LinkedIn also has a section for Skills where some of these certifications may appear to fit. Your decision here is to choose where you want this specific piece of experience to fall in your LinkedIn Profile since Education is closer to the top of the page than Skills. Since most people reading this book will read Profiles from top to bottom, this is something to consider.

Recommendations: As already mentioned, this is the one section on your Profile where you allow *other people* to talk about you, which is helpful if the messaging is tailored to your current target market. You may have dozens of LinkedIn Recommendations, but I suggest only showing a few of them publicly at any given time. Why would you do that? Think about who, aside from your mother, would take the time to read the good things that 22 people have to say about you. It is often helpful to select three to five Recommendations that resonate most with your current target market and display those. For some useful tips on giving and receiving Recommendations, take a look at Chapter 7.

Websites: LinkedIn gives you the opportunity to direct your Profile viewers to the external websites that mean the most to you. This feature allows you to drive traffic to your business, a nonprofit you support, or any other site on the web. Make the most out of this opportunity and always select "Other" when given the choice to name your URLs. *RockTech: LinkedIn Adoption* is much more compelling than the generic *My Company* option. This will also increase the search engine optimization (SEO) value of the websites that you choose to display.

Twitter: LinkedIn partnered with Twitter in late 2009 to give you the option to link your Twitter account to your LinkedIn Profile. Since these two tools have fundamentally different target markets for most people, I normally recommend putting the link to your Twitter handle in your LinkedIn Profile but suggest not having your every tweet appear in your LinkedIn status. If you tweet more than you think your professional network would want to see in their Network Activity, they may hide the messages you'd like them to see. Conversely, many professionals find it useful to send most, if not all, of their LinkedIn Status Updates to Twitter from this feature.

Public Profile: Described in more depth in Chapter 10's Privacy and Security considerations, your Public Profile is the version people see when they're not logged into LinkedIn and perform an online search for you. As I explained in the previous chapter, LinkedIn allows you three different options for how much information is shown here (Figure 10.4).

Generally, I recommend making all your information public but inserting only the data about yourself that you want the world to know.

LinkedIn also gives you the option to personalize the URL to your Public Profile, instead of having an alphanumeric code at the end of your URL that looks something like this:

www.linkedin.com/in/david-gowel/8/68b/3b3

You can create your own URL that both looks more professional and contributes to your SEO value, as seen here:

www.linkedin.com/in/davidgowel

Once you create your personal URL by entering your first and last name without spaces (if your name is a popular one, such as John Smith, you may need to add a middle initial or an acronym that people may associate with you), you may want to consider adding it to your e-mail signature block. This is a helpful way for you to subtly send out more detailed information about yourself when corresponding with your target market.

Summary: Here you have the opportunity to speak to your audience, describing who you are and what you do well. It is common for people to copy and paste a résumé, speaker bio, or other third-person account of what they have accomplished into this section. However, the most interesting and useful Profiles don't follow this copy and paste methodology. A well-written summary should leave the reader with the feeling that they have just had a conversation with the person whose Profile they are viewing. People prefer connecting when a LinkedIn Profile offers not only details about their professional focus, but also a sense of their personality. For this

Summary

I'm proud to work with an exceptional team and set of advisors at RockTech. Our flagship product, the Technology Adoption Platform (TAP) for LinkedIn is a productivity tool that allows our target market of relationship-driven professionals to adopt LinkedIn so they can generate warm leads, shorten sales cycles and close deals.

Using the leadership and management skills gained as a US Army Ranger / Veteran of the Iraq War, I seek to enable RockTech's strategic goals through partnerships with exceptional teams and professionals. If interested, some of our clients' ROI-based testimonials are showcased in my recommendations below.

In addition to the time I spend focused on growing RockTech, I also support various non-profit organizations with my primary efforts surrounding the East End House as well as military and wounded warrior causes.

Specialties

Ethical leadership
LinkedIn strategy
Technology Adoption Platform (TAP)
Solving problems using new technology
Public speaking & teaching
Team building

For LinkedIn search effectiveness, I'm commonly mistaken for Dave Gowell, Gallo, Growell and Brad Pitt.

Figure 11.4   Sample Profile Summary

reason, it is preferable to use first-person prose in a professional tone for your Summary, as long as you feel your target market would respond positively. An example of my latest Summary is shown in Figure 11.4.

Specialties: This section is especially appealing to military-minded folks like me who want the quickest and most concise answer to everything. The Specialties section allows you to enter keywords that describe the most valuable aspects of what you do. Are you a talented public speaker? Do you know software revenue recognition or generally accepted accounting principles (GAAP) better than anyone else out there? Let your target audience know about it in terms that they might use when searching for someone like you.

Current and Past Positions descriptions: You will want to carefully tailor these brief but important summaries to your current target market so that you can alert your network to exactly how your past positions have helped prepare you for what you are (or hope to be) doing for them now.

A Note about Groups: Many people gravitate toward LinkedIn's Groups feature without first knowing how to use

LinkedIn. Strangely enough, this popular and valuable element of LinkedIn has distracted many users from the platform's true value. This is why effective group usage is considered a more Advanced feature and, ironically, the Advanced People Search is a feature that all users should learn early on. Although potentially powerful, if used outside of a thoughtful strategy, LinkedIn's Groups can become a time-intensive distraction from the underlying power of this platform. It can be very tempting to spend much time searching for, participating in, or building and managing groups with the thoughtful functionality LinkedIn has built in this area. However, a goal of this book is to allow you to learn how to use LinkedIn's unprecedented social business intelligence in the real world. Therefore, I'm going to refrain from an explanation on the ins and outs of Groups to keep from distracting you here, as well. For more information on groups, visit http://learn.linkedin.com/groups/.

Personal Profiles at a Collective Level

The greatest value that can be gained from LinkedIn is not through individual use but through organized use by many collaborative individuals seeking to achieve a common goal. A key element to this approach is that you can't have the latter without the former. The need for each individual Profile to nest comfortably within a corporate strategy is the first step to success. Business leaders who seek victory in this realm are then forced to recognize and align first with the interests of their employees, not the other way around. This is also an appropriate idea to consider, as individual LinkedIn account mastery leads to an organization's employees having a deeper understanding of LinkedIn, which makes them better armed to contribute to corporate strategy.

LinkedIn's most basic building block is the personal Profile. Company pages, Groups, and Advanced People Searches all ultimately derive their utility from that core element of business: the individual. But when individuals gather their LinkedIn prowess and choose to organize their efforts toward enabling a commonly sought-after business goal, unprecedented synergies abound. Despite the individual focus in this platform, LinkedIn is a professional tool, so we can't ignore corporate ramifications when setting out to protect or establish your brand. To demonstrate the significance of this approach, think of LinkedIn as an orchestra. Individual musicians playing their respective instruments in separate theaters may sound flawless when apart. When placed in the same environment, the absence of the conductor tying them together results in nothing more than unpleasant noise. So it is with individual employees doing similar jobs in the same company: If they don't project complementary messages in LinkedIn, it just sounds bad.

Now let's take the musical metaphor into the next stanza to consider your target market. Even if all the members of your symphony play harmoniously and the conductor is beaming with pride, you won't keep the playhouse seats full if that tune is classical when your audience was expecting to hear jazz. Similarly, your company needs to ensure that both your senior leaders and target market are mesmerized by the harmonious message your employees project in order to maximize LinkedIn's personal Profile effectiveness. Individual employees can use their job descriptions to enter specific keywords or phrases that emphasize—to both human beings and search engines—the areas in which your business excels or wants to compete.

Just as it is a conductor's responsibility to ensure that the audience gets what it came for, it's a leader's responsibility to return to those two magic words when crafting corporate LinkedIn strategy: target market. And it's not enough to *tell* employees what to copy and paste via a boilerplate paragraph established by the marketing department, as people can sense (and will often recoil from) a redundant sales pitch. Employees should be educated on how LinkedIn can be helpful not only to them but also to their organization. Furthermore, they should become aware of which key concepts or themes the organization desires to project, while being permitted to tie in their personal value proposition to their specific target market.

Finally, remember that LinkedIn is only a single tool, and part of its effective strategic implementation requires that you know when to step out of this tool and integrate it with others. The key here is to ask yourself what you need to do to make this a successful piece of the strategy within your business. Three important elements that should be taken into consideration when integrating LinkedIn are your firm's personalities, software, and human systems.

One of the reasons that many large companies succeed is that a diverse mesh of personalities and skills work together toward a collective goal. However, with this benefit comes complexity. Your CFO, John Outdated, might argue, "I'm a successful professional, and I've *been* successful *without* LinkedIn for my entire career." Although he might see the value in it, it isn't enough to convince him to spend the time learning the tool. Many people have preconceived notions about LinkedIn; and even if some see that it's useful, they're just not going to use it. Or maybe Mr. Outdated just isn't technologically savvy and doesn't fully understand *how* to use it. Either way, it's necessary to consider the fact that he may have an incredible network, and if he's left out of your corporate LinkedIn strategy, it may result in a grand underutilization of social capital for your company as well as that individual.

Most people already have incredibly valuable stores of social capital at their disposal that they are unable to cash in on, simply because they haven't connected to the right people on LinkedIn and learned to use effective searching mechanisms to discover it. Instead of coercing the unwilling but well-connected teammates to create Profiles and build networks, we often suggest having them delegate these tasks to a LinkedIn assistant who may be someone who manages their other professional affairs. If done effectively, this type of proxy usage can tap deeply into previously untapped networks. For example, an assistant could draft a Summary and print out all of the Invitations received for Mr. Outdated. Then while he's sitting in an airport waiting to board a plane, Outdated can quickly read and edit the proposed Summary and highlight the Invitations from people who he knows that he wants his assistant to connect with on his behalf. Proxy usage takes many forms and grows more effective (yet more complex) when dealing with ultra-high-powered individuals with vast networks. It is advisable in this type of situation to employ team-proxy tactics. Develop a consistent standard for sifting through the tremendous amounts of business intelligence, taking it from the mind of the executive or celebrity and inserting it into software platforms that can more effectively share it with other members of the organization to their benefit.

Integrating LinkedIn with other software you already use is an easy way to keep track of your connections' most recent information. As explained in the next chapter, the Export Contacts feature allows you to upload a .csv file (this stands for comma separated value, and it will appear similar to an Excel spreadsheet) into different Customer Relationship Management (CRM) software platforms. Since it's far more likely that your connections will update their own information more often than you will do it for them, you're now in possession of the most recent contact information for your connections, even while logged out of LinkedIn.

Integrating LinkedIn with your human systems of behaviors involves understanding your sales cycle, HR processes, corporate culture, and business practices, as well as determining where LinkedIn best fits into the mix. Taking the time to understand where the tool is an amplifier and where it can be a distracter is critical to your success.

Now that we've examined how to protect the privacy of your network and how to project the best message personally and collectively, we'll explore the key considerations for how you should grow that network, including the best (and worst) methods of doing so.

Chapter 11 Summary

- LinkedIn's value lies more in how it works than in how it looks. However, a certain degree of etiquette compliance in your Profile allows you to achieve an acceptable level of completeness as perceived by your target market, especially when compared to your competitors. You should keep the following two things in mind when creating your Profile: your target market and projecting your desired level of professionalism.

- By tailoring your Profile to appeal to your target market, you can provide opportunities for useful incoming correspondence.
- For a company to effectively use LinkedIn, it's essential for all of its employees to collaboratively use their LinkedIn networks for personal and collective corporate success in an organized fashion.
- Groups are best used only after the true value of LinkedIn is mastered.

12

Effective Network Growth

As NEW TECHNOLOGY emerges, so do different categories of users—each with their own adoption traits. According to Rogers' Technology Adoption Life Cycle Model, the five major adopter categories are Innovators, Early Adopters, Early Majority, Late Majority, and Laggards.[1] The Innovators are, not surprisingly, the risk takers; they're the first to adopt and typically the youngest. They are followed by the Early Adopters, Early Majority, and then the Late Majority. The Laggards take the backseat and are usually skeptical, conservative, traditional people who resist change (this is the hesitant adopter who would likely have typed this book on a typewriter while taking breaks to saddle up and ride his pet triceratops for a coffee break). It takes each subsequent category longer than the previous one to adopt a new technology and is generally done so with the following percentages of total population being assigned to each category. Figure 12.1 shows the distribution curve for technology adoption.

Following the model in Figure 12.1, let's place some numbers next to these percentages, based on LinkedIn's assessment that there are 500 million professionals in their target market[2]:

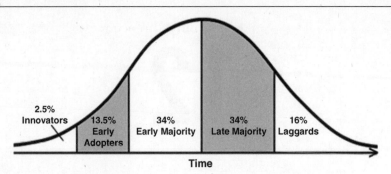

Figure 12.1 Technology Life Cycle Model Adoption Curve

Figure credit: Katie Berdan

Innovators	12.5 million	
Early Adopters	67.5 million	(cumulative: 80 million)
Early Majority	170 million	(cumulative: 250 million)
Late Majority	170 million	(cumulative: 420 million)
Laggards	80 million	(cumulative: 500 million)

This model fits neatly with LinkedIn's stages of usage—at first. But this book is designed to reset that curve. Most Innovators and Early Adopters used LinkedIn but confused it with social media. They applied communicative social media habits to LinkedIn's features, which they should have instead used to carry out more disciplined business intelligence activities.

To use a metaphor (which, as you've realized by now, is something I love to do) to describe this misuse of LinkedIn, let's imagine that LinkedIn is a shiny, new Ferrari—and that your real-world network is the fuel that you put into this exotic sports car. It will purr like a kitten when you fuel up with the high-octane gas (your real-world network) in the tank. However, if you put in the lesser-grade petrol (a diluted network where you accept all invitations), the car will still run—just not as well as it could otherwise.

If you've never had access to high-octane power before and you chose to cruise with the bad gas for some time, you probably wouldn't know you aren't getting all you can out of the car (or LinkedIn). Eventually, your engine becomes clogged and too difficult to maintain (like your LinkedIn account when you have too many connections). It may just become a decoration for your driveway (which is about as useful as LinkedIn would be if it were truly just "Facebook in a suit") instead of something that can take you places you've never been before, and fast. Furthermore, if you use quality fuel but don't put enough of it in the tank (have too few connections), your engine won't even start, forcing you to only sit and look at a gorgeous automobile (which is what many users do if they just focus on Profile beautification in LinkedIn and forget to connect to all of their real-world connections).

This inappropriate Ferrari maintenance is similar to what Rogers' Innovators and Early Adopters have done with LinkedIn. They simply didn't recognize the strategic value that LinkedIn could provide them at that time. There are two key factors that now make LinkedIn as powerful as a Ferrari that were not present the first (or fiftieth) time many of these individuals started using this platform:

1. LinkedIn had to have enough user Profiles in its database to allow people to connect with enough of their actual real-world connections to start mapping their 2nd and 3rd degree networks.
2. Each user not only had to have the ability to connect to a large number of their real-world contacts via LinkedIn but actually had to take the time to connect to them.

Without satisfying these two criteria—something physically impossible for most of the Innovators and Early Adopters—it wasn't possible to experience the quietly growing power of LinkedIn. However, it is possible now. The problem we face today is that those Innovators and Early Adopters who led the pack of good-looking but relatively slow-moving Ferraris onto the highway ended up taking a wrong exit. The rest of the Early Adopters and the Early Majority are set to follow their tail lights down the same (wrong) road. To put this situation in numerical context, at the time of publishing this book, LinkedIn is targeting nearly another

350 million users, who have not yet signed up for a profile, and are all postured to misuse the tool if they don't hear this message.

When I first started writing *The Power in a Link*, LinkedIn had about 70 million users. This means that if you're reading this book within the first few years of its publication (under current growth projections), the Early Majority has still yet to wake up to the tool. What does this mean for you? Well, if you start using LinkedIn effectively now to properly grow your network, the third "P" in our "4P" methodology, you will likely outpace your competition. Specifically, you will do this with the ability to directly stimulate word of mouth to the market share for which you're competing. This chapter is meant to help the Innovators and Early Adopters find the on-ramp that will guide them back onto the highway of success. I also want to keep the rest of the Early Majority, Late Majority, and the Laggards from following an erroneous path. It's the *quality* of the network contacts that you add to your LinkedIn account that determines your effectiveness, since the *quantity* of opportunities is already there for many markets—waiting for you to seize them.

In early 2009, LinkedIn saw many users driving their Ferraris toward this erroneous exit at lightning speeds. In order to avoid a catastrophic loss of value to their platform, they capped the number of people to whom a user can connect at 30,000. They realized the site's overall user experience would be irreparably damaged if everyone automatically connected to everyone else. If LinkedIn was made up of falsely connected individuals, the genuine, useful links would be indistinguishable, and most of the potential business intelligence would be drowned out by noise.

Let's look at a tangible example of having a low-octane versus high-octane network. Let's assume John WannaKnowYa is a 2nd degree connection of mine, indicating that one or more individuals in my network are connected to WannaKnowYa, as shown in Figure 12.2.

In this example, because I have real-world relationships with Jane CubicleChum and John CollegeFriend, I have the likely opportunity to earn a warm introduction to or gain business intelligence about my target market (John WannaKnowYa) by using LinkedIn.

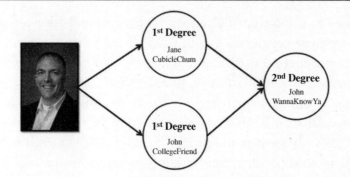

Figure 12.2   My Network With High-Octane LinkedIn Connections

On the other hand, had I connected with four people I only loosely know who fall between me and my target (as demonstrated in Figure 12.3), LinkedIn would only provide me ineffective information for getting me to WannaKnowYa. This situation most commonly occurs when people connect to others for reasons that do not provide compelling business value (some are represented by the fictional names of my hypothetical 1st degree connections in Figure 12.3).

This example illustrates why super-connecting can be a tremendous waste of valuable time, time that *could* have been spent requesting a potentially successful warm introduction from a friend or colleague.

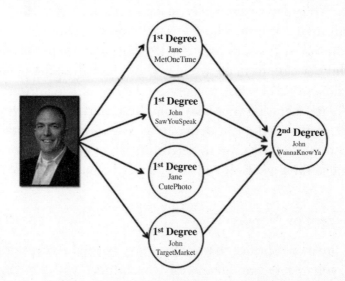

Figure 12.3   My Network With Low-Octane LinkedIn Connections

Keep in mind that if CollegeFriend's personal connecting policy is to super-connect, I would figure it out quickly when I asked for an introduction to my target and he could not introduce me to or provide any information on him. In this situation, I might take the time to craft a well-thought-out note to CollegeFriend explaining how an introduction to WannaKnowYa would be mutually beneficial only for him to tell me, "Sorry, I don't know him. I connected to him because we shared a LinkedIn Group and he had an interesting background." So while I may still personally like CollegeFriend, I would probably choose to remove him from my LinkedIn network—or at the very least, discount his potential relationship with any connections that I identify as being interesting to me. CollegeFriend would be providing me noise, not value, so I'd devalue any apparent wealth of social capital he may want to project in LinkedIn.

It is a best practice to connect with people who pass your deliberate litmus test, whatever that may be. As a general rule, you should connect to people with whom you have rapport, people you're confident would comfortably give you at least one of the two things mentioned above: an introduction or business intelligence. The litmus test you use to determine what invitations you accept will be unique to you. You may occasionally make exceptions regarding whom you will invite or from whom you will accept invitations. For new LinkedIn users, this can be a challenging (and sometimes uncomfortable) decision to make while wading through social nuances in this online world of selecting Connect, Ignore, or Disconnect.

When generating your own litmus test, start by identifying your current professional goals, derive from that your target market, and then use that information to determine who you'll invite or accept to achieve those goals. It will be well worth your time to do so.

To Accept or Not Accept

There are more options that you can take beyond Accept or Ignore when you receive an invitation to connect with someone on LinkedIn. What should you do if you get a message from someone whose name you don't recall? If at first glance they don't pass your litmus test, there are a few extra steps that allow you to determine if this is a good case to approve an exception to policy:

1. **The message:** You might receive a personalized message from this person ("Hey, we talked at this conference about XYZ, and I'd like to hire you for your services . . . "), or you may get the standard message ("I'd like to add you to my professional network"). Some people don't like the standard message because it lacks personalization. Although this *can* make an invitation seem less sincere, it is often acceptable to use the stock message when sending invitations. The justification for this is that the person should know you well enough that your name is all that is needed to identify you as a trusted contact. If you feel you need to write a crafty or thoughtful message, perhaps this person is not someone with whom you should connect just yet. A second reason the nonpersonalized message is common is because (as we discuss throughout this book) LinkedIn is not used widely by most professionals as a communications tool . . . yet. Important communications should come through means your target market currently uses: phone, text, e-mail, meetings, golfing, at a game, or anywhere the members of your target market are most comfortable communicating. If you don't know me, then you can get to me through my gatekeepers (my 1st degree connections), if you know them. LinkedIn's greatest current strength is that it's a phenomenal business intelligence and network mapping tool. Therefore, you may not want to ignore those invitations that don't personalize a note; just move on to step two.

2. **The picture:** Does this individual look familiar? You probably meet a lot of folks at conferences or networking events, and if you're one of those who never forgets a face, someone who favorably impacted you may be recalled this way if you didn't get her card (this also reinforces the need to put your picture on LinkedIn). If her mug shot doesn't ring a bell, take step three.

3. **"How you know this person":** LinkedIn usually compels you to specify how you know users to whom you request to connect

(you have the option of choosing things like friend, colleague, classmate, or group affiliate). This can help jog your memory or at least bring it up to a brisk walk. If still drawing a blank, go to the last step.

4. **The Profile:** Click on the link that takes you to his or her Profile (keep in mind that if you do this and your Profile Views setting is in anything other than stealth mode, that person may get some information about you). While viewing the inviter's Profile, first look to see if you have any mutual connections (this is the step that triggered the series of events leading to my relationship with Major League Baseball star Curt Schilling). Is this person in my target market? Can they provide value for me or vice versa?

Now that you have dug a little deeper into this invitation, you have some options:

- **Accept** this person into your network.
- **Ignore,** which removes the invitation from your inbox without sending that person a notification.
- **Reply without accepting,** so you can probe further into the intentions of the initiator without allowing him or her into your 1st degree network.
- **Report as Spam,** which allows you to report any suspicious, unsolicited, or harassing activity.
- **Do nothing.** You have other ways to spend your time—and a full inbox doesn't destroy the value of LinkedIn.

Remember that if you accept someone whom you don't know into your network, you also give him access to your e-mail addresses. Ignoring someone is equivalent to giving him a cold shoulder: the request stays in his sent messages, and he may believe that you just haven't come across his invitation yet. You also have the option to report his message as spam, yet another feature that makes LinkedIn a self-correcting ecosystem that allows us to report harassment as it occurs.

If you don't know the person but believe that she could potentially be a fit for something you are working on, you can choose to reply by saying something like, "Hey, how do we know each other? I apologize if my memory is failing me!" or use another similar canned message that you store in an easily accessible folder that you just copy and paste for such situations. If this person doesn't know you or had no mutually compelling reason to connect, she may just not respond to your reply. Because you've crafted a com-pelling message through your Profile and have connected to many people you know well, you should be prepared to be found in searches by people with whom you may actually want to explore such opportunities. If that's the case, the incoming marketing ele-ment of LinkedIn is working for you.

Now that you're armed to defend yourself in the case of an un-invited attacker or are disciplined to *hold your fire* upon a potential bearer of good news, we move on to discussing some ways in which you can most effectively grow your network.

Network Growth Best Practices

There are several ways to invite people into your network. It's helpful to find the methods that are most comfortable for you, as one of your goals should be to most expeditiously reflect your real-world contacts as connections in LinkedIn. If you know a specific person with whom you want to connect, a simple people search will do. Figures 12.4 and 12.5 show the steps you would take if you were looking to connect with me.

(If you actually *know* me in a manner that fits our mutual litmus tests, continue on. If you don't know me and you choose to send me an invitation, a "Who are you?" message may head your way.)

The most expedient method of network expansion lies within the green Add Connections link at the top right of any page on LinkedIn. Clicking here will serve up a page where the tabs at the top allow you to add Colleagues, Classmates, and People You May Know. This is another reason why it's helpful to list all of your prior jobs in your Profile, because this option brings up the col-leagues that worked at those organizations at the same time you

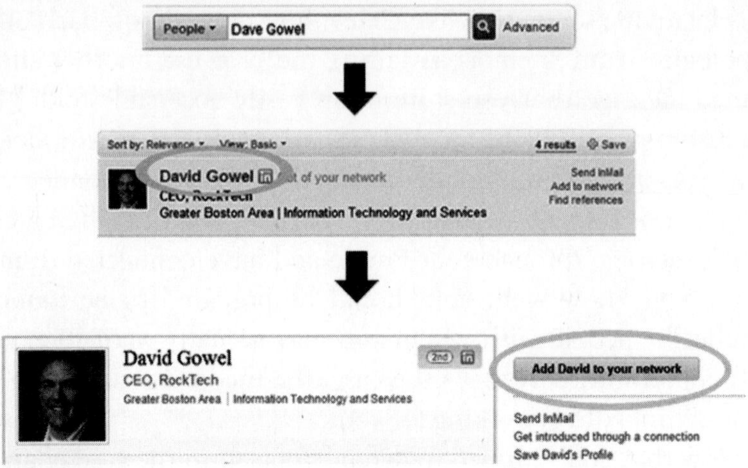

Figure 12.4   How to Connect to Someone

worked there . . . only if you listed those positions and time frames in LinkedIn. If you don't list a position, you will not have past colleagues suggested to you as easily, nor will your name be suggested to them to invite you.

Figure 12.5   How Do You Know This Person?

The People You May Know feature causes intrigue for those who wonder how LinkedIn knows the people you may know. The simple explanation is that LinkedIn uses an unpublished algorithm, which apparently considers mutual connections along with your current network and other data that the platform finds relevant in order to generate suggestions for you. Although you don't have to connect with those on this list, it's a very helpful tool for finding people you may know.

Finally, to help your real-world network more quickly become reflected by your LinkedIn network, use the See Who You Already Know on LinkedIn feature. This tool allows you to import the e-mail addresses you saved from people you e-mail in Outlook, Apple Mail, Gmail, Hotmail, Yahoo, AOL, and many other webmail providers. If you use a desktop e-mail application, be sure to first click on the green "Add Connections" link at the top right of every page, then click the link at the bottom of the blue box at left that reads "Import Your Desktop Email Contacts".

You can either import your contacts directly from your e-mail client (if you use Microsoft Outlook), or you can upload a contact file that has been exported from your e-mail client and saved as a .csv, .txt, or .vcf file. If you choose the first option, it will ask you to download an ActiveX Control, allowing LinkedIn to review the contacts in your Outlook address book and let you know which of those contacts are already on LinkedIn.

After uploading, you will have the option to invite these people into your network. LinkedIn may posture you to invite all of your contacts to connect, so the first thing to do is uncheck the Select All box at the top left of your contact list. If you were to click Invite when every one of your imported contacts was selected, this would send an invitation e-mail to everyone (possibly including those *not* on LinkedIn) asking them to connect with you. This is probably *not* what you want to do, especially if you have many contacts who aren't yet LinkedIn users. It's generally preferred that you check only the names of relevant people who are currently using LinkedIn. These names, when in blue, also serve as hyperlinks that will take you to view their Profiles. If a name is in black and cannot be clicked, then that person is not using Linked-In (or they have not assigned that e-mail address as one they use on LinkedIn).

Because you probably have more than a dozen or so contacts (I've seen clients who have many thousands), this list will be saved in your Imported Contacts section of LinkedIn. If you choose to invite some contacts to join your network while saving others for later, you can always come back to this Imported Contacts section. And once you've uploaded these contacts, you will get a notification on your home page and a suggestion to connect with that person if at any point in time someone in your Imported Contacts joins LinkedIn, registering the e-mail address that you have saved for them.

So for example, let's say you upload 6,000 e-mail addresses into LinkedIn, and it tells you that of those 6,000, about 1,000 of them are in LinkedIn already. The rest of those 5,000 e-mail addresses will be saved in your account. If Jane NewUser is one of those 5,000 and she later joins LinkedIn using the e-mail you have for her, you may get that notification of her entry into LinkedIn in your Network Activity on your home page. This is yet another reason to have all the e-mail addresses assigned to you (work, personal, alumni, and so forth), associated with your LinkedIn account. If John YouSeeker has your Hotmail e-mail address, but you only assign your work and Gmail e-mails to your LinkedIn account, YouSeeker may not be able to find you. This has led many users to become afflicted with a type of LinkedIn schizophrenia, because people who want you to join LinkedIn (John YouSeeker) may then send you an invitation to connect via your Hotmail e-mail address that you don't have associated with your primary account. When you accept this person's invitation, it creates a new account for you, using your Hotmail account as the primary address. Then new connections seeking you may find either one of your accounts, sending further invitations to connect to your alter ego. You can easily close an extra account while logged in under that account in your Settings page.

At this point in the discussion, it's important to note the difference between the terms *contact* and *connection*. Your contacts are

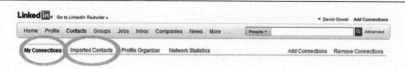

Figure 12.6 My Connections and Imported Contacts

those e-mail addresses that you've uploaded from your e-mail providers' address books, whereas a connection is someone who is in your Network (1st, 2nd, or 3rd degree). Figure 12.6 shows the LinkedIn screen that contains both My Connections as well as Imported Contacts.

Some people reading this may have their jaws on the floor, thinking, "I'm not uploading my Rolodex onto the Internet!" But before you go all crazy-eyed and throw something at me, hear me out. Even when you put this information into LinkedIn, nobody but you can see the contacts you've uploaded. LinkedIn does not give away the names of, sell to, or harass those individuals. The goal of this feature is to provide you with an easier method of having your real-life network reflected as best you can in your Linked-In network. When the connection is made, the tool becomes extraordinarily useful, as you can see from the things I've done and am doing with it.

My Best Invitation to Connect . . . Ever

There is one pre-LinkedIn social capital investment that I made while still a West Point cadet that is hands down the highest return trade of my life. The story below demonstrates how I rapidly built and used social capital (in the absence of sufficient real capital) with many people throughout Boston over a six-month period whom I initially didn't know in order to convince my girlfriend to become my wife.

It was the summer of 2001, and my then-girlfriend had made a comment about the newly built high-rise Ritz Carlton property that came into view over Boston Common as we

(continued)

(*continued*)

drove through the city that day. "Hmm, I wonder what the rooms look like up there. . . . " That one sentence set forth an explosion of rapidly firing synapses in my brain, as I was about to enter my Firstie (senior) year and was seeking the best way to pop the question.

Between that car ride and December 28, 2001 (also known as Game Day), I launched a social capital campaign. I came up with a plan and aimed to include four of the finest hotels in Boston. During my monthly trips to Boston, I would get up for morning runs and secretly go to these hotels and supporting businesses to propose, negotiate, and coordinate my plan. I could have just called and set this all up remotely if I had real capital to pay them for their services, but the scheme I lay out below cost me less than $1,000 (don't worry, Honey, that doesn't include the ring). I was only able to pull this off by building social capital with people I didn't know through hard work, persistence, sincere verbal gratitude, and a dash of romance. I executed an outside-the-box way to think of building and using social capital for situations where hard capital isn't available.

So here's how the big day played out from my target market's perspective: She woke up around 8:00 A.M., expecting to meet me for lunch in Boston. So she was surprised when, at 10:00 A.M., a long black limousine picked her up at her apartment with a dozen long-stemmed roses on the back seat (thanks to Bruce at Boston Rose Flower Shop) and a note saying:

Julie, on the bottom of this are directions;

unless he knows how to get there, give him (the

limo driver) this card. He'll take you to the Park Plaza

in this car. Then, take these roses to the front desk . . .

(Note: If you placed the first letter of each line of this and the follow-on notes in sequence, it read, "Julie I love you. Will you marry me?")

Upon arrival at the Park Plaza Hotel, Julie was met by the hotel manager, escorted up to the presidential suite, and told, "There's something in here for you that you need to find." Upon searching the room, she found another dozen roses and a card that led her to the next hotel—the Four Seasons. Upon arrival, she was met by the hotel manager, who happily walked her up to *their* presidential suite. When he opened the double doors to the room for her, she found a card propped up on a chair, leading her to another card and dozen roses in the master bath, which led to *another* card and dozen roses under the grand piano, which led to the *final* card with another dozen roses and gold necklace on the balcony overlooking Boston Common (I made her work for that one).

The card with the necklace led her to the Hotel at XV Beacon. Once she found the card there, she got back in the limo, and finally, she was taken to that new Ritz Carlton about which she had been pondering over six months previously. On arrival, she was met by the manager and walked to the final presidential suite of the day. Upon opening the door on that cold December morning, the fire was burning and single long-stemmed roses were laid in a path, leading Julie around the gorgeous view overlooking Boston Common, while classical music played throughout the room. Following this trail to the master bedroom, she found her future Linked-in Jedi in a white tuxedo (one that the concierge had to help said college student figure out how to put together) with his hands behind his back. As she began running to me, I stopped her in her tracks by getting down on one knee. And finally channeling a wealth of social capital provided to me by what felt like half the city of Boston, I delivered a very concise yet compelling message to *Request a Connection* . . . and she didn't select *Ignore*.

Two more features that will aid your network growth are the Export Tool and Connection Surfing. The latter allows you to browse the connections of your 1st degree connections (unless they choose not to allow anyone to see their connections via privacy settings). If you are viewing the Profile of someone you know well, you can surf his connections to find a mutual acquaintance whom you haven't yet invited into your network. Or you may find someone whom you don't know but might like to, which could prompt you to ask for an introduction (if you have enough social capital built up with this person).

Finally, once you have accurately replicated your real-life network on LinkedIn, you can choose to export your contacts to a .csv file. This option is somewhat hidden at the bottom right corner of the My Connections page. When you click Export Connections, you will get a list of all of your contacts' most recent, self-updated information downloaded to your computer, where it can then be uploaded to your CRM, e-mail marketing, or other software.

Your network is the fuel that gives you better, relationship-filtered search results and makes your target market more likely to find you. So, once you've enabled your LinkedIn account with that high-octane network, your Ferrari will be ready to roll, and you'll be postured to gain the intended benefit that this book provides: you'll know how to use LinkedIn to build your own social capital, stimulate relationships, and generate business.

Network Shrinkage

So what do you do if you have already connected to hundreds, thousands, or tens of thousands of people you don't know?

First, create your litmus test and stop connecting to people whom you *don't* know. Then use the Export Connections tool described in the previous section, which will allow you to hold on to the e-mail addresses for all those people to whom you have already connected. This step will make the next one more emotionally tolerable for some, because it's time to "vote people off the island."

Many users incur significant frustration once they understand that the way they have been doing business is not the best way to continue using LinkedIn. It's not easy for them to see their connections number go from 15,000 to 150. Yet . . . this *should* be a no-brainer based on the previous discussion regarding the ineffectiveness of a low-octane network (if not, at least you'll have the e-mail addresses for all those folks saved from the previous step, in the event that you want them later.)

Once you're ready to remove connections that you have made in the past, simply click the main menu option for Contacts and then click Remove Connections on the top right of the screen. It is here that you can select individuals from whom you would like to disconnect by clicking in the check box adjacent their name, and then clicking Remove Connections on the right side of the page when ready to disconnect. Keep in mind that those whom you remove as a connection will not be notified that they have been removed, they will only be able to recognize that they are no longer a 1st degree connection if they view your Profile.

So the LinkedIn landscape is now set for its users' success (at least those who have read this book):

1. We now have the Innovators and Early Adopters back on the *right* highway.
2. The Early Majority are warming up their engines in their driveways.
3. The Late Majority are trying to find their LinkedIn car keys.
4. Those unfortunate Laggards are still waking up in their beds with Model Ts in their garages . . . but we're hoping they've seen the light and are considering Ferrari shopping later this year.

For those who are ready to hit the gas, let's see just how fast your jet fuel-filled Ferrari can take you when you cruise around your network looking to pick up your target market in a much easier way than you ever have before.

Chapter 12 Summary

- The emergence of new technologies creates different categories of users, each possessing its own traits of adoption. This technology adoption life cycle model can be applied to LinkedIn to demonstrate the logic behind its original users' misuse of the tool.
- There are two factors, not available when LinkedIn first emerged, that are necessary to make LinkedIn the powerful tool it is today:
  1. LinkedIn had to have enough users in its database to allow people to connect with enough of their actual real-world network to start mapping their 2nd and 3rd degree connections.
  2. Each user not only had to have the *ability* to connect via LinkedIn but actually *had to connect* to a significant number of his or her real-world connections.
- If you get into LinkedIn and start using it effectively now, you will increase your chances of outpacing your competition, as you will have the ability to directly stimulate word of mouth to the market share for which you compete.
- It is important to realize that it's primarily the *quality* and not the *quantity* of the network contacts you add to your LinkedIn account that leads to business success. However, some degree of quantity is required to have "enough gas in the tank."
- Creating your own litmus test for deciding with whom you will connect is helpful in saving time while connecting or searching.

13

Business Tools

In Search of Good Company

As we've already discussed how to use LinkedIn's Advanced People Search (Chapter 4)—arguably one of its most valuable features when tied to a strategy and an effectively grown network—it is helpful to review another feature that LinkedIn offers to help you reach your target market (operating under the guidelines of proactive business tool usage—the fourth and final "P" in our "4P" methodology). It is inevitable that you will be looking to find an organization at some point in your life, be it to sell to, partner with, get hired by, or acquire. The revolutionary aspect of LinkedIn's Company Search (you can think of it as an organization search, as it includes noncorporate entities as well) is that it allows you to get a snapshot of the organizations in your network, sorted by relationships you have within those organizations. For example, if you search for a company like RockTech in the Company Search area, you'll receive corporate data, much as you would in your web search engine of choice. But instead of only results showing corporate data such as location of the headquarters or a general product

Companies › RockTech

Overview Careers Products Analytics

This page was last edited on 09/05/2011 by Christy Schmidt   Admin tools ⁻

RockTech | RockTech integrates LinkedIn and other social technologies into your business practices through our proprietary Technology Adoption Platform (TAP). Through TAP, we provide training that is relevant, measurable and scalable for clients seeking to leverage misunderstood social platforms. We change ... more

RockTech has **64** followers

✓ Following ⁻   Share

How you're connected to RockTech

18 First degree connections

4 Second degree connections

22 Employees on LinkedIn

Check out insightful statistics about RockTech employees »

Your Network (22)   New Hires (2)   Employees (22)

CEO
David Gowel, Greater Boston Area

Investor
Eric Solem, Greater Boston Area

Director
Scott McCabe, San Francisco Bay Area

Figure 13.1   Example of a Company Page

and services overview, LinkedIn results also include relationships you have or can get to in that company, as shown in
Figure 13.1. However, this will only be the case if you've followed the best practices laid out in this book.

A valuable feature of the Company Search is that you are able
to see which companies in your network are hiring. This can be
useful when you are job hunting or looking for companies in
growth mode for any number of reasons.

Figure 13.2 shows that you can access this feature by hovering
your mouse over Companies in the main menu, then clicking
Search Companies in the pop-up menu, and finally clicking the
Search Companies tab at the top of the page.

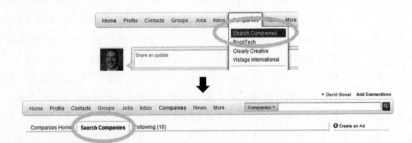

Figure 13.2   Clicking on the Companies Tab

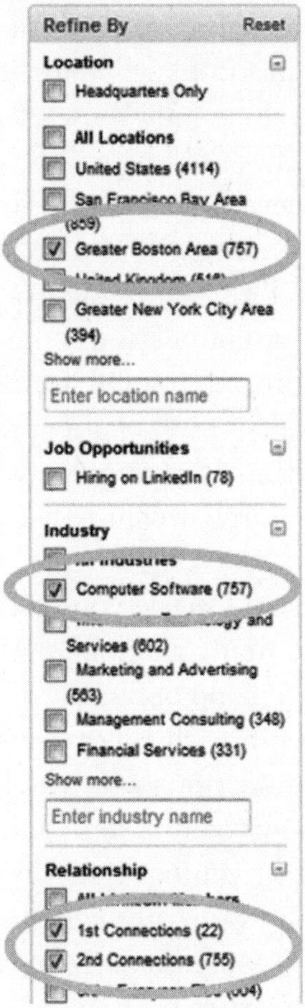

Figure 13.3   Options for Refining Your Company Search

This tab will allow you to adjust various criteria to focus your search so that you can be surgically precise in dissecting your network to reveal relevant companies in your search results. Let's illustrate with an example (a search for the following use case is demonstrated in Figure 13.3):

Perhaps you're a partner at a law firm and are seeking computer software companies in the greater Boston area who may need your legal services. You are looking specifically for companies that employ people whom you or your connections know, because these are individuals who you can most easily reach to get intelligence on that company or help shorten your sales cycle by having an existing relationship refer you. Selecting 1st and 2nd degree connections will simplify your search, because you'll get results that include only those closest relationships.

Keep in mind that these results will be different for every person because they are viewed through the lens of each user's individual network. These results will also change over time even for you, as more company Profiles are created, as you connect with more people, and as your connections connect with more people. Having a robust network leads to more fruitful searches, so if you're not getting many results, review the previous chapter which discusses network growth. My current network yielded 775 results when performing the search we just discussed. What did yours yield?

LinkedIn also offers you suggestions on a side panel in its faceted search: once it sees that you chose certain options, it proposes to you other options to expand or narrow down your search.

Your results may begin with several companies that have the names of 1st degree connections who you know in that company (at least, you *should* know them if you connected to them). These 1st degree connections (if you have any in these results) are most useful when someone in your network with whom you've lost touch moves into a new company unbeknownst to you. The more impactful result from this search often occurs when you have 2nd degree connections within a company. Though you won't know anyone there (yet), you *will* know someone who has a relationship with an employee there. Depending on the quality of the connections you accept or invite (your high-octane fuel) into your network, you'll be able to request business intelligence about—or perhaps even an introduction to—an influential member of that company through your 1st degree connection.

Now that you see how LinkedIn searches are quite different from those you may perform via search engines, you should be able to appreciate how this tool has many more layers of functionality than you likely initially thought. Let's move to discussing more deeply some ways to leverage the information from LinkedIn, especially when you're no longer logged into LinkedIn.com.

When to Link Out

Requesting introductions is an act that many of the most traditional and private LinkedIn users are less likely to perform through LinkedIn's functionality. It is culturally too far ahead of its time for this influential subset of the business world . . . for now. Therefore, this is a time when it might be preferable to "link out" and communicate where you expect your target market to be more comfortable: in person, via e-mail, via conference call, or at a dinner, an event, the golf course, and so on. In general, of all the options available, e-mail is often the easiest option to request an introduction. This e-mail should tactfully request the recipient's advice on whether there would be mutual benefit from an introduction to the target you have in mind. If yes, then it makes sense to do what you can to make that introduction more comfortable for your contact to send to your target. This is counterintuitive to many sales- or marketing-minded professionals who find directly approaching their target to be the fastest way to reach them. However, the time-saving nature of first earning a warm introduction from a mutual connection you share with that target comes into play when that introduction removes the barriers often raised by your target when she receives a cold call, e-mail or sales pitch. The social capital used to introduce you can make all the difference between being warmly received instead of facing a cold shoulder.

Many people struggle to find their style for requesting introductions via e-mail, so I offer the example shown in Figure 13.4 as one way to send a note to a contact, when asking for an introduction.

Regardless of the style you choose in requesting introductions, it is helpful to consider these guidelines:

- **Since you are asking for a favor, make granting that favor as easy as possible.** By providing your bio, or even proposing the entire introduction, you lessen the burden of the introduction because your contact doesn't need to spend time writing it himself. In the example in Figure 13.4, Steve is now armed to introduce me more quickly and in a way that focuses on the message I want Jeff to receive.

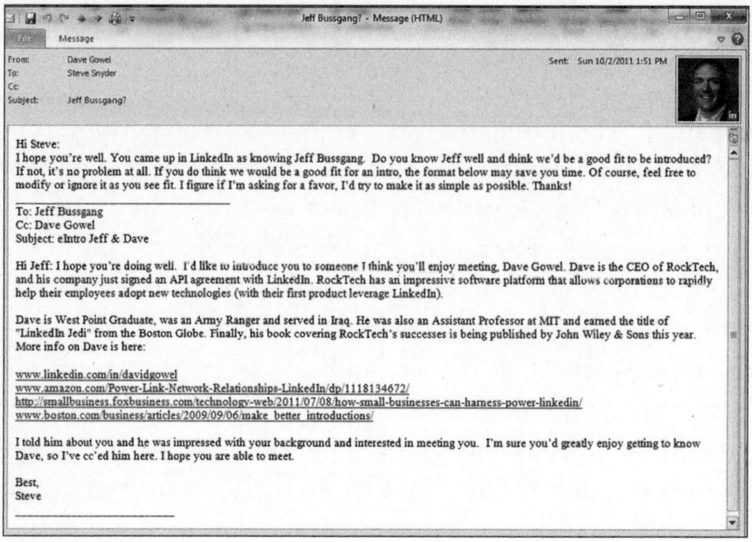

Jeff Bussgang? - Message (HTML)

Message

From: Dave Gowel
To: Steve Snyder
Cc:
Subject: Jeff Bussgang?

Sent: Sun 10/2/2011 1:51 PM

Hi Steve:
I hope you're well. You came up in LinkedIn as knowing Jeff Bussgang. Do you know Jeff well and think we'd be a good fit to be introduced? If not, it's no problem at all. If you do think we would be a good fit for an intro, the format below may save you time. Of course, feel free to modify or ignore it as you see fit. I figure if I'm asking for a favor, I'd try to make it as simple as possible. Thanks!

To: Jeff Bussgang
Cc: Dave Gowel
Subject: eIntro Jeff & Dave

Hi Jeff: I hope you're doing well. I'd like to introduce you to someone I think you'll enjoy meeting, Dave Gowel. Dave is the CEO of RockTech, and his company just signed an API agreement with LinkedIn. RockTech has an impressive software platform that allows corporations to rapidly help their employees adopt new technologies (with their first product leverage LinkedIn).

Dave is West Point Graduate, was an Army Ranger and served in Iraq. He was also an Assistant Professor at MIT and earned the title of "LinkedIn Jedi" from the Boston Globe. Finally, his book covering RockTech's successes is being published by John Wiley & Sons this year. More info on Dave is here:

www.linkedin.com/in/davidgowel
www.amazon.com/Power-Link-Network-Relationships-LinkedIn/dp/1118134672/
http://smallbusiness.foxbusiness.com/technology-web/2011/07/08/how-small-businesses-can-harness-power-linkedin/
www.boston.com/business/articles/2009/09/06/make_better_introductions/

I told him about you and he was impressed with your background and interested in meeting you. I'm sure you'd greatly enjoy getting to know Dave, so I've cc'ed him here. I hope you are able to meet.

Best,
Steve

Figure 13.4 Example of Asking for an Introduction

- **Naturally, your connections may want to tweak your comments or include their own.** This guideline allows your contact to flavor your messaging by the relationship he has to your target connection. It's important to let him feel comfortable changing what you say about yourself as he may not be comfortable with some of the language you propose.
- **Give the recipient an easy way to decline.** Say something like, "Do you think this person and I would work well together?" If you were, in fact, a bad fit for whatever reason, you wouldn't want to make your contact feel awkward about declining to make the introduction, causing him to then avoid you. In my example, Steve may not know Jeff well, or any number of other reasons could exist for him wanting to say "no."

Because Steve accepted me into his LinkedIn network and my social capital had grown with him through our positive interactions, I was able to not only learn that he knew Jeff Bussgang but also *earn* that introduction. Then since I proved Steve's suspicion correct (that Jeff and I would get along well, as was clear in our first meeting at Flybridge), a few key things happened:

1. Steve's social capital account increased with me, because he made an introduction for me that I requested.
2. Steve's social capital account with Jeff increased, because Jeff was pleased enough with that first interaction to hire my company.
3. Since both Jeff and I owe Steve social capital for simply using personal judgment to make the introduction, an anomaly in capital trading has just occurred: the absence of a loss for all players involved. There is no downside for anybody in this equation. Steve, Jeff, and I all end up with a greater benefit. The only loser in this exchange was my competition who didn't use LinkedIn to get in the game and therefore didn't have a chance at earning Flybridge as a client.

In a nutshell, this example demonstrates the power of LinkedIn: It's all about making our professional lives more productive. This is a tool that provides us with access to exponentially greater utility from the relationships we have today. The fact that LinkedIn can provide you with the information needed to easily stimulate these introductions is game changing. The existence of these types of exchanges (that happen every day *outside* of LinkedIn) supports the revolutionary value that LinkedIn has the ability to create tremendous global business value. This is when LinkedIn becomes the breeding ground for this value-based trade where everybody wins (those who know how to use, and not abuse it, of course).

In making our professional lives more productive, this book focuses primarily on the power available in using the free tools LinkedIn provides to individuals. However, professionals often ask about certain elements of LinkedIn's premium offerings. Notably, *LinkedIn Recruiter* is a business-to-business (B2B) product sold to those members of LinkedIn's target market who are responsible for finding and hiring top talent. This product provides its purchasers unlimited search access to all of LinkedIn's user profiles. *Recruiter* has a host of helpful tools for organizing and sharing recruiting projects and targets within an enterprise-level organization and, until recently, these enterprise tools have only been available for use in recruiting.

In September 2011, *LinkedIn for Salesforce* was released. This tool, for the first time, integrates LinkedIn's precious relationship and self-populating professional information with a Customer Relationship Management (CRM) tool with, in this case, Salesforce.com. The significance of this new offering demonstrates that LinkedIn has an interest in supporting job functions outside of human resources. For all those thinking LinkedIn is only a competitor to Monster.com, CareerBuilder, or other job sites, consider all the job functions that could benefit from a stronger ability to amplify relationships. As LinkedIn continues to spread its wings in the professional world with tools such as *LinkedIn for Salesforce*, it's apparent that momentum is only growing for this social network. Notably, however, the building blocks that empower any enterprise offering from LinkedIn gain their validity from effective individual use of LinkedIn's free service.

Chapter 13 Summary

- The revolutionary aspect of LinkedIn's Company Search is that it gives you a snapshot of the Companies in your network, sorted by relationships you have within them, *if* that search is based on your true, real-world network. Your search results include who you personally know, or who you can get to through who you know, in each company.
- Another valuable feature of the Company Search is that you are able to see which Companies in your network are hiring. This can be useful when you are job hunting or looking for companies in growth mode that you'd like to sell to, partner with, and so on.
- If you are asking for an introduction, consider doing so in this manner: Make it as easy for your introducer as possible; let your introducer feel comfortable changing what you propose in a template or bio that you provide; and make sure you give your introducer an easy way to decline your request.

- The existence of social capital transactions (happening every day outside of LinkedIn) supports the revolutionary value that LinkedIn provides its users. LinkedIn, when used properly, provides unprecedented data that allows professionals to generate more of those transactions, more efficiently.
- *LinkedIn Recruiter* and *LinkedIn for Salesforce* are premium tools that help professionals to use LinkedIn's data in an enterprise offering.

14

The World at Your Fingertips

If You Give a Man a Fish

As discussed in the Introduction, in order to take advantage of this powerful business tool we first have to carefully focus the lens that will allow us to peer into our networks for the information we desire. This starts by overcoming your privacy and security concerns. If those worries still linger while you are clicking around in LinkedIn, it's likely that you'll be hesitant to discover its full potential.

After gaining comfort in your privacy and security, you then have to ensure that the message you (and your organization) project is compelling to those in your target markets. If this is a halfhearted or unrefined message inserted just to check the block for having a LinkedIn Profile, it's unlikely to resonate with your target audience.

Finally, it's vital to enable your search capabilities with that well-grown network before searching or implementing corporate strategy. If it's too large or not large enough, your network is either diluted or has untapped potential. If it's too professional, LinkedIn won't know to inform you that your cousin's neighbor is a CEO in your target market. If it's too personal, your network will exclude members of your company who would stand to gain from making a key introduction to you, but they will continue to be ignorant of the potential power they have now. Until you have begun to clearly map your complete real-world network and then methodically expand it, the results you earn will reflect your efforts: garbage in, garbage out.

The guiding principle shaping this process of making sure your LinkedIn Privacy Settings, Profile, and Network are all up to par boils down to this: even though LinkedIn is a disruptive technology, it is not most effective as a stand-alone tool. Without using it properly and in concert with the other software, systems, and personalities that affect you, LinkedIn can very well be (and is currently, for many), just Facebook in a suit. Also, if you don't take the time to manage your relationships in the real world, LinkedIn will only show you people who are unwilling to provide you warm introductions or those unlikely to share with you the valuable business intelligence you seek.

The importance of following the methodology in this book became apparent to me as early as my initial experiences in teaching LinkedIn. During Clearly Creative's early years, I delivered 30- to 60-minute LinkedIn presentations to groups where attendees would then say, "Wow, I can't believe how powerful that tool is. It's amazing!" However, when I reviewed those attendees' Profiles 30 days following each presentation, I would see that they rarely updated their Summary, added any significant number of connections, or uploaded a professional photo. Why not? It's because my session consumed the single hour per month that they normally devoted to LinkedIn, as well as any *other* social media. They understood the features and even the potential benefits but failed to realize the mechanics required for the behavior change needed to leverage this tool effectively. They became distracted from trying to achieve this by the other demands in their lives. Only through behavioral change will LinkedIn yield the win-win-win situations that people like Jeff, Steve, and I now understand and enjoy.

If You Tie a Fishing Rod to His Hand and Handcuff Him to a Boat

So even if we play on the previous section's title and *teach a man to fish*, that is still not enough to utilize the greatest potential from LinkedIn. Effective LinkedIn usage is not something you can hire a consultant to do for you (giving you a fish), or even take a one-off training class to master (teaching you to fish). It's about displacing your current wasteful behaviors by methodically using LinkedIn to accomplish goals that you could never achieve without it (teleporting the fish into the boat).

One intelligent and successful client of ours, John About-ToRetire, articulated the challenge in changing behavior best when he said, "I can see the value and understand why I should be using LinkedIn. I'm just not going to; I'll let the rest of our firm do it."

Why would he say this? Is he trying to hurt his brand or that of his company? Does he *want* his business to fail? No. Not from what I've seen when personally consulting on LinkedIn to thousands of people in just about every industry and seniority level. His attitude stems from a simple fact: humans are creatures of habit. If you've spent a career meeting exceptional success, changing your ways to adopt something that appears unnatural to you is not an easy shift.

This book was written as a way to show the world something that it hasn't quite grasped yet: The power of LinkedIn. My journey was one worth telling in these pages because my story goes a little like this: I began my career as a soldier who then entered civilian life as a young, disconnected, inexperienced entrepreneur opening a business in an atrocious economy. It was my avid and thoughtful use of LinkedIn that allowed me to earn the respect of a time-honored, globally renowned business brand while partnering with LinkedIn, one of the most cutting-edge technologies on the planet. Now my company helps corporations of all sizes to change the behavior of their employees through a software platform I couldn't have built if my LinkedIn expertise wasn't good enough to find the incredible team to build it, investors to finance it, and clients to buy it. I know it can do the same for your personal and professional goals, and hope you will embrace it as I did.

LinkedIn provides information about the otherwise invisible relationship map around you that you cannot get anywhere else in the world. And now that you know this truth, you should attempt to make this tool unique to you by integrating its content (which is impossible for you to generate outside of LinkedIn) into the other tools you use on a daily basis. LinkedIn provides unprecedented and indisputably valuable information to which you gain access by mapping your network and searching for the people you seek. When you integrate this untapped resource of information into the rest of your professional life, the results are incredible.

This platform is not the be-all and end-all tool. Some successful people are not going to stop using Rolodexes, just as many will always keep a death grip on their paper calendars. And that's fine. LinkedIn is best used to augment, not replace, all of your current methods of doing business. You will start to find success with LinkedIn where you recognize specific and comfortable use cases within your recurring activities.

So where is LinkedIn going from here? It's going everywhere. It unlocked itself for business technology integration in late 2009, when it opened its API.[1] This open doorway allows for the integration with other software tools that you are already using and is the mechanism through which RockTech launched its platform.

LinkedIn will change the way we do business forever. Other platforms that are based on LinkedIn's database of Profile information (and the web of relationships within) will certainly arise, but it's unrealistic to think that we are going to repopulate that information anywhere else. The way that it's connecting efficiency with accuracy, and accessibility with untouched information is arguably more valuable than any tool we've had available in business previously. LinkedIn will modify and improve some of our most accepted business practices.

Do you recall when I asked you to think about a world where you can find the clients, employees, investors, service providers, and business partners you seek by using, not abusing, valuable, trust-based relationships?

Wake up. It's here.

Notes

Chapter 1

1. Wikipedia, accessed August 19, 2011, http://en.wikipedia.org/wiki/Social_capital
2. Robert Putnam, *Bowling Alone: The Collapse and Revival of American Community* (New York: Simon & Schuster, 2001).

Chapter 2

1. Merriam-Webster, accessed August 19, 2011, www.merriam-webster.com/dictionary/media.
2. LinkedIn Company Page, accessed August 29, 2011, www.linkedin.com/company/linkedin/products.
3. Scott Morrison, "LinkedIn Wants Users to Connect More," *The Wall Street Journal*, accessed December 29, 2009, WSJ.com.
4. LinkedIn Press Center: Press Releases, accessed August 29, 2011, http://press.linkedin.com/98/linkedin-secures-53m-funding-led-bain-capital-ventures.
5. Reuters, accessed August 29, 2011, http://www.reuters.com/article/2011/05/19/us-linkedin-ipo-risks-idUSTRE74H0TL20110519.
6. Jeffrey Bussgang, *Mastering the VC Game* (New York: Portfolio, 2010).
7. R. Hoffman and M. Pincus, *U.S. Patent No. 6,175,831* (Washington, DC: U.S. Patent and Trademark Office, 2001).

Chapter 3

1. SpringerLink search page, accessed August 19, 2011, www.springerlink.com/content/p73r842rr5586656/fulltext.pdf, page 16.
2. If you visit my Profile, you'll notice that I am a paid member of LinkedIn. There are two reasons for this: (1) I saw that there were certain clear

benefits for my upgrading; and (2) to competently advise our clients, our business compelled us to know how to use the paid features, as well as the free version. There are many benefits to upgrading your account, but those LinkedIn users (paid or unpaid) who actually know how to use this platform in the way I suggest throughout this book are the ones who get exponentially more value than those who do not.

Chapter 4

1. As of when *The Power in a Link* was written.

Chapter 8

1. http://press.linkedin.com/98/linkedin-secures-53m-funding-led-bain-capital-ventures.

Chapter 10

1. Clayton Christensen's home page, accessed August 19, 2011, www.claytonchristensen.com.
2. Reid Hoffman's LinkedIn page, accessed August 19, 2011, www.linkedin.com/in/reidhoffman.
3. LinkedIn's Help Center, accessed August 19, 2011, http://linkedin.custhelp.com/cgi-bin/linkedin.cfg/php/enduser/std_adp.php?p_faqid=42.

Chapter 11

1. LinkedIn featured the reference to this success in their 100 million-user marketing campaign in March 2011.

Chapter 12

1. The technology adoption life cycle model was developed by Joe Bohlen, George Beal, and Everett Rogers. Rogers first published a book on the theory, *Diffusion of Innovations*, in 1962.
2. Jeff Weiner Interview with CNNMoney, accessed August 29, 2011, http://money.cnn.com/video/technology/2010/03/25/tm_linkedin_weiner_ceo.fortune/.

Chapter 14

1. Adam Nash's LinkedIn blog, *LinkedIn Platform Open for Business*, accessed November 23, 2009, http://blog.linkedin.com/2009/11/23/linkedin-platform-launch.

Acknowledgments

THIS BOOK FOCUSES on the power of relationships and it was a warm introduction that opened the door for me to have this book published by John Wiley & Sons. It's also important to note that this literary victory would not have occurred without a loyal group of my 1st degree relationships who collaborated, critiqued, encouraged and energized me to live through—and then write about—the experiences in these pages. Sincere thanks to my friends, family members, advisors, teammates, investors, clients, and critics.

Within my enormous support brigade, the actions of a few individuals shined brightly throughout the entire process. First off, Christy Schmidt eagerly accepted the challenge and contributed tremendously to this effort. Her organization and editing of the stories and lessons, coupled with her research skills and passion to keep us on time and on target, helped deliver the product you have before you.

The love of my life, Julie, with whom I cofounded Clearly Creative. She eased the burden during my transition into civilian life while she became a mother of an epic caliber and then was a teammate in birthing this book. Julie oversaw the editorial process from the day I first put fingers to keyboard, up until a year later when we signed the contract with John Wiley & Sons. She's amazing in more ways than I can count.

Led by Shannon Vargo, the team at John Wiley & Sons is an elite unit of literary professionals. Their expertise, patience, and entrepreneurial understanding provided me insights and flexibility for which I could not be more thankful.

Finally, these people know what they've done for me, this book, and for my professional evolution. Your efforts, time, counsel, critiques, and much more will not be forgotten:

Roger Staubach	Joe Ryan	Oscar Jazdowski
Tim Glenn	Bob Matson	Garth Rose
Anita Grisham	John Chory	Todd Cieplinski
John J. Gowel	Mark Rockefeller	John Sabino
Kate Gowel	Jose Fernandez	Bob Alperin
Gregg Fairbrothers	Sasha Grinshpun	Mark Gallagher
Bill Aulet	Marty Coyne	Stephanie Carter
Jeff Bussgang	Jane Johnson	Steve Snyder
Scott McCabe	Adrian Talapan	Emily Mendell
Deborah Schindlar	Eric Solem	Janet Lehman
Elana Schulman	John Snyder	Jada Den Herder
Richard Foote	Brian Ranaudo	Matt Svetich
Anne Smith	Jenny Ranaudo	Jack McCullough
Adam Young	Detlef Rethage	Marcella Cheung
Damian Wisniewski	Phil Francis	Al Chase
Sarah Gallop	Steve Mannell	Scott Kirsner
John Allen	Tony Martin	Dick Dube
Marsh Carter	Dan Allred	Amos Oh
Abby Bratt	Jeff Glass	Mike Gonnerman
Laura Salema	Deep Nishar	Elizabeth Lim
Martha Richardson	Jerry Shereshewsky	Jim Boozer
Joe Guidi	Nate Bride	Gary Speer
Dawn Irons	Peter Kurzina	Mike Tucker
Mark Lohr	Howard Anderson	Jim Murphy
Joni Lohr	Ken Morse	Betsy Murphy
Eric T. Johnson	Laura Morse	Eric A. Johnson
Andrew Bialecki	Steve Vinter	Katie Berdan
Kevin Potts	Tom Clay	

And last but not least (except in age), Charles David Gowel.

Index

For complimentary access to tools that will allow you to implement the strategies demonstrated in this book, go to

www.rocktech.com/powerinalinktools